WILD GOD

WILD GOD

40 DEVOTIONS FOR ADVENTURE, RESILIENCE, AND FAITH IN THE WILDERNESS

Creek Stewart

BakerBooks
a division of Baker Publishing Group
Grand Rapids, Michigan

Published by Baker Books
a division of Baker Publishing Group
Grand Rapids, Michigan
BakerBooks.com

Printed in the United States of America

Library of Congress Cataloging-in-Publication Data
Names: Stewart, Creek author
Title: Wild God : 40 devotions for adventure, resilience, and faith in the wilderness / Creek Stewart.
Description: Grand Rapids, Michigan : Baker Books, a division of Baker Publishing Group, [2026] | Audience term: Christians
Identifiers: LCCN 2026003179 | ISBN 9781540905710 cloth | ISBN 9781493456628 ebook
Subjects: LCSH: Devotional calendars | Nature—Religious aspects—Christianity | LCGFT: Devotional literature
Classification: LCC BV4811 .S834 2026
LC record available at https://lccn.loc.gov/2026003179

Cover illustration and design by Stephen Procopio

Baker Publishing Group publications use paper produced from sustainable forestry practices and postconsumer waste whenever possible.

26 27 28 29 30 31 32 7 6 5 4 3 2 1

INTRODUCTION

Have you ever felt an unexplainable pull toward nature? Have you noticed how time spent in the wild seems to clear your mind, calm your spirit, and awaken something deeper within you?

For years, I misunderstood this connection. I thought it was simply about getting fresh air, disconnecting from screens, or pushing personal limits. But I've come to believe something far more profound: God is wild.

From the very beginning, He designed the wilderness as a place for us to draw closer to Him. That's why creation still calls us today. It's not just the call of the wild. It's the call of our Creator.

Genesis 2:7 tells us: "Then the LORD God formed a man from the dust of the ground and breathed into his nostrils the breath of life, and the man became a living being." God could have formed the first human in a palace or temple, but He didn't. He formed Adam from wilderness soil and placed him in a garden. The wilderness was humanity's original sanctuary. And, as Genesis 3:8 reveals, God was right there with them: "Then the man and his wife heard the sound of the LORD God as he was walking in the garden in the cool of the day, and they hid from the LORD God among the trees of the garden." Throughout Scripture, we see the wilderness used by God not as a punishment but as a place of preparation, purification, and profound encounter.

Deuteronomy 8:2–6 explains that God led the Israelites into the wilderness to humble them, test them, and teach them to depend on Him:

> Remember how the LORD your God led you all the way in the wilderness these forty years, to humble and test you in order to know what was in your heart, whether or not you would keep his commands. He humbled you, causing you to hunger and then feeding you with manna, which neither you nor your ancestors had known, to teach you that man does not live on bread alone but on every word that comes from the mouth of the LORD. Your clothes did not wear out and your feet did not swell during these forty years. Know then in your heart that as a man disciplines his son, so the LORD your God disciplines you.

David fled to the wilderness, caves, and deserts. Here, he wrote some of the most heartfelt psalms in the Bible, such as Psalm 63:1: "You, God, are my God, earnestly I seek you; I thirst for you, my whole being longs for you, in a dry and parched land where there is no water." Matthew 4:1 tells us that even Jesus "was led by the Spirit into the wilderness," where He fasted, was tested, and prepared for His public ministry.

Again and again, the wilderness becomes sacred ground and a place to draw closer to the Lord. The wilderness strips away our distractions. It reminds us of our dependence, and it reveals the beauty, power, and provision He has embedded in His creation.

As a wilderness survival instructor, television host, and author, I've spent most of my life teaching people how to survive in harsh environments, make fire, find shelter, purify water, and identify edible plants. But along the way, I found myself lost in the wilderness of life. Ironically, I found my way back home by learning to see and draw closer to God in the wild.

I've come to believe that survival and wilderness skills weren't just discovered by early humans. I believe they were *given* by the God who hardwired provision into the plants, animals, rocks, and everything else in creation. Even when Adam and Eve were banished from the garden, God didn't abandon them. He clothed them. He provided. And He still does for us. Romans 1:20 says it like this: "For since the creation of the world God's invisible qualities—his eternal power and divine nature—have been clearly seen, being understood from what has been made, so that people are without excuse."

Creation tells the story of the Creator. That's the heartbeat of this devotional. It's a collection of forty wilderness-themed reflections that blend survival and outdoor skills with biblical truth. Each one is rooted in Scripture and born out of personal experience, from deep forests to desert canyons and from mountaintops to valleys. My hope is that these devotionals will inspire you to seek God in wild places both physical and spiritual.

As a full-time survival instructor, I meet a lot of armchair survivalists. These are people who read the books, watch the videos, and binge the survival TV shows, but who never step into the wilderness to get their hands dirty and truly practice the skills. Untested skills can't be trusted when they matter most. Each entry includes action steps like Scripture contemplation, wilderness journal questions, daily prayer, and hands-on wilderness applications. These will press you to live out the truths of the devotional in your daily walk with Christ so you don't settle for becoming an armchair Christian. These aren't just feel-good devotionals. They'll ask you to dig deep and get dirty. Just like with wilderness survival skills, getting dirty prepares you for when things go sideways.

Whether you're in a literal forest or a season of life that feels like a wilderness, God is near. He is still revealing Himself through creation. And when you quiet your soul long enough to listen, you'll hear His voice and see His provision in the rustling leaves, the crackling fire, and the wind on your face.

Over the years, I've come to believe that the wilderness isn't just a backdrop, it's an invitation, a classroom, a sanctuary, and a proving ground for your faith. And more than anything, the wilderness is a place to encounter the wild, sovereign God who created it all.

And maybe one day we'll meet around a campfire. I now host WILD GOD weekends, where we combine hands-on survival training with honoring the God who hardwired these resources and provision into creation.

If your heart is stirred by what you read here, consider this your invitation to learn more at WildGod.org. I'd love to see you in the wild.

WILD SURVIVAL SKILLS

In almost every one of my survival classes, someone eventually says something like this:

"I wonder who the first caveman was to rub two sticks together?"

Or . . .

"I wonder who the poor guy was who ate poison hemlock for the first time?"

It's human instinct, and common practice, to assume that the foundational survival skills we know today, like fire starting, hide tanning, toolmaking, and sourcing cordage from plants and trees, were discovered at random by early humans somewhere along the line. It's what the educational system teaches us—that ancient people stumbled upon the secrets of survival through trial and error, like seeing who died after eating the wrong mushroom or somehow discovering that striking iron pyrite against flint could create a spark that could ignite a very specific fungus that's been boiled in ash water.

There's no doubt that humans are creative and adaptive. But I want to challenge the status quo with a wild idea: What if those original survival skills didn't come from humans at all? What if they came from the Lord?

Let your mind wander with me back to the beginning.

What happened when Adam and Eve disobeyed God and did the one thing He asked them not to? Genesis 3:17–24 tells us plainly:

> To Adam he said, "Because you listened to your wife and ate fruit from the tree about which I commanded you, 'You must not eat from it,'
>
> "Cursed is the ground because of you;
> through painful toil you will eat food from it
> all the days of your life.
> It will produce thorns and thistles for you,
> and you will eat the plants of the field.
> By the sweat of your brow
> you will eat your food
> until you return to the ground,
> since from it you were taken;
> for dust you are
> and to dust you will return."
>
> Adam named his wife Eve, because she would become the mother of all the living.
>
> The LORD God made garments of skin for Adam and his wife and clothed them. And the LORD God said, "The man has now become like one of us, knowing good and evil. He must not be allowed to reach out his hand and take also from the tree of life and eat, and live forever." So the LORD God banished him from the Garden of Eden to work the ground from which he had been taken. After he drove the man out, he placed on the east side

of the Garden of Eden cherubim and a flaming sword flashing back and forth to guard the way to the tree of life.

I believe the Bible is 100 percent true. I believe it's 100 percent inspired by God. And I believe every single sentence is in there for a reason.

As a wilderness survival instructor, I can't help but wonder, Did God let Adam and Eve watch Him make their garments from skins? Did He teach them how to make clothing from hides?

What I love most about this moment is that just because Adam and Eve disobeyed doesn't mean God stopped loving them, or that He stopped providing for them. It doesn't mean He turned His back for good. But it did mean they were going to have to survive in a new way, in a new land, as Genesis 3:23 describes: "So the LORD God banished him from the Garden of Eden to work the ground from which he had been taken."

They no longer had the protection of the garden. They no longer had divine provision growing effortlessly in the garden around them. They now had to work to survive. But they needed to learn these new skills. And they were dependent on someone teaching them.

Maybe tanning hides into buckskin was Survival Skill #1, taught by the world's first, best, and most qualified wilderness survival instructor: God Himself.

When Adam and Eve left Eden, there was no Walmart, no Home Depot, and no Hobby Lobby. Every tool, every container, every fire, every shelter, every article of clothing would need to be made from scratch. And who better to teach them than the One who hardwired every natural resource on earth with intention and purpose?

That's what blows me away. As I study and teach survival skills, I can't help but see divine fingerprints in everything. I believe the Lord loves it when we marvel at His creation, whether it's a mountain or a mushroom, a sunset or a snakeskin. It honors Him to stand in awe.

But what's even more amazing? God engineered a Plan B into creation. He designed the wild to sustain us and provide for us, even after Eden. From metal and cotton to hot sparks and food, everything we need is already here. We just need to know where to look.

I don't believe early humans figured out these foundational survival skills by random on their own. I believe, as Genesis alludes, that they were taught by the One who put it all here in the first place. And sadly, so many of these God-given survival skills have been lost to history. Some have been preserved by Indigenous cultures and passed down for generations, but far more, I imagine, are gone forever.

I look forward to one day rediscovering these skills in the classroom of heaven, taught by the original survival instructor. How awesome it will be to watch as He pulls back the veil on creation and shows us all the cool survival tools, resources, food, medicine, and more that He engineered into the soil, plants, trees, rocks, animals, bugs, and everything else in the wild. And what's even more humbling is that He not only made it all, but He made it all for us and will never stop loving us.

God doesn't do anything at random, and nothing on this earth is accidental. Everything He put here has a use, function, and purpose. And all of it points to a sovereign Creator.

When people read the story of Adam and Eve, they tend to focus on the fact that God kicked them out of the garden, as if it were a point of abandonment. But what many people fail to meditate on is the first thing God did for them outside of Eden: He provided.

I love this about our God. Never, since the very first day of human history, has He given up on us. Everything in creation is here not only to help us see Him but to reveal that His love is engineered into the wild.

God is literally wild!

IN THE WILD

Verse to Contemplate

The LORD God made garments of skin for Adam and his wife and clothed them. (Gen. 3:21)

QUESTIONS FOR THE WILDERNESS JOURNAL

1. Have you ever thought of survival skills as something God may have originally taught?
2. In what ways has God provided for you, even after a mistake or failure?
3. What part of creation fills you with awe or wonder about God?
4. How can you depend on God more fully in your everyday life?

PRAYER OF THE DAY

God, thank You for never leaving us, especially when we don't deserve Your provision. Thank You for embedding provision in Your creation and for being the original source of every survival skill and every good gift. Help me to see You in the wilderness, to depend on You like Adam and Eve had to, and to marvel at how deeply You've thought through every detail of this wild and beautiful world. In Jesus's name, amen.

WILDERNESS APPLICATION

Choose one primitive survival skill, such as fire starting, hide tanning, or cordage-making, and study it through the lens of divine engineering.

Ask:

- What natural materials are needed?
- How might God have designed these materials for this purpose?
- How does this skill reveal His creativity and provision?

Then go out and practice it prayerfully and gratefully, marveling at what He's made.

WILD RESCUE

For over two decades, I've been called upon by countless news outlets, podcasts, morning shows, and blogs, all asking me the same question: "What should someone do if they're lost in the wilderness?"

My answer is always simple, yet it's something most people struggle to follow:

1. Admit you're lost.
2. Stop moving (don't try to self-rescue).
3. Put up a rescue signal.
4. Wait for the rescue crew.

Human nature pushes us to keep moving, as we think that we can walk our way out if we just try harder. But from my experience on the television show *SOS: How to Survive*, where I've studied dozens of real-life survival stories, this approach often leads to exhaustion, panic, injury, and even worse decisions. Self-rescue when you're lost can become a vicious cycle of making things worse.

I've seen it time and time again on my show: people trapped in survival situations, believing that their effort alone will save them, only to find themselves more lost, more exhausted, and more desperate. But what if I told you that I found myself in a similar situation—lost—not in the wilderness, but in life? If only I listened to my own advice.

Several years ago, at the height of my career, I had everything I thought would fulfill me: multiple published books, several television shows, and recognition as a survival expert. But none of it satisfied me. Behind the scenes, my life was falling apart. My marriage was on the brink of collapse, I wasn't living at home, and there were divorce papers on the table. I was lost, not in the woods but in the wilderness of life.

I was chasing all the things the world told me would bring fulfillment—success, achievement, and material gain. But none of it brought me the clarity or peace I desperately needed. I was just like those people on my show, trying to self-rescue, only to find myself more broken and more isolated. It took rock bottom for me to finally admit that I couldn't save myself, no matter how many things of this world I chased.

I'll never forget that moment. I was holding my infant son, River, while he cried in my arms. I caught a glimpse of myself in the mirror, and all I felt was shame. It was then that I heard God say clearly, "I made you to be a better man, a better father, and a better husband." I fell to my knees and finally sent up a rescue signal to the only One who could truly save me: Jesus.

I prayed: "If You want this marriage to work, You're going to have to fix it. I've tried everything. I can't do this on my own anymore. I surrender my marriage to you."

Although I had grown up in church and was "saved" at fourteen, this was different. It was the first time I truly surrendered any part of my life to God's will. And just like that, Jesus met me in my wilderness. As 2 Corinthians 4:18 reminds us: "So we fix our eyes not on what is seen, but on what is unseen, since what is seen is temporary, but what is unseen is eternal." I stopped focusing on the temporary achievements of this world and sought God's perfect will. It wasn't easy, and it didn't happen overnight, but Jesus saved my marriage. It's hard to explain with the limited words of this world. He healed wounds, released bitterness, and helped my wife Sarah and me fall in love again in ways we never thought possible but always wanted. God's rescue was real, and His restoration was complete.

Just like those lost people on my television show, it took hitting rock bottom for me to finally admit I couldn't self-rescue. And I know I'm not alone. Many people are wandering in the wilderness of life, flailing in their own strength, unaware that rescue is just around the corner if they surrender to Someone who knows exactly how to rescue.

Rescue requires courage to do the following:

1. Admit the path you're on isn't working.
2. Surrender to a Rescuer with a proven track record—Jesus.
3. Put up your rescue signal through prayer.
4. Trust the Rescuer to do the work.

There is nothing that Jesus can't redeem. As Romans 8:28 promises, "We know that in all things God works for the good of those who love him, who have been called according to his purpose."

No circumstance is too dire, no valley too deep, and no mountain too high for Him to climb. As Psalm 139:7–8 reminds us, the Hound of Heaven will not stop until he finds us right where we're at: "Where can I go from your Spirit? Where can I flee from your presence? If I go up to the heavens, you are there; if I make my bed in the depths, you are there."

It's easy to get turned around and think we can figure it out on our own. But self-rescue in life is impossible. The world's promises will never satisfy. They will always leave us empty and in need of real sustenance.

IN THE WILD

Verses to Contemplate

Where can I go from your Spirit?
  Where can I flee from your presence?
If I go up to the heavens, you are there;
  if I make my bed in the depths, you are there.
    (Ps. 139:7–8)

QUESTIONS FOR THE WILDERNESS JOURNAL

1. Is there any area of your life where you've been trying to self-rescue?
2. What does putting up a rescue signal look like for you spiritually?
3. Can you think of a time when you fully surrendered a situation to God? What happened?

4. In what ways are you still holding on to control, even after experiencing God's rescue in another area?
5. How might your current wilderness season be preparing you for restoration?

PRAYER OF THE DAY

Father, I admit that I've tried to rescue myself too many times. I've wandered and worked in my own strength, only to end up more lost and worn out. Thank You for being a Rescuer who never gives up on me. Help me surrender fully, not halfway. Shine Your light on the areas I've tried to control and meet me in my wilderness once again. I trust You to find me, to restore me, and to lead me home. In Jesus's name, amen.

WILDERNESS APPLICATION

- Go on a short solo hike or spend time alone outside in silence. Find a quiet place and reflect: "In what areas am I spiritually lost right now?"
- Bring a mirror with you (or use your phone camera). Look at yourself and ask: "What am I really chasing?" Take time to be honest with God and send up a rescue signal in prayer.
- Sketch or write about your own wilderness experience—what it felt like, where it led you, and how God met you there.

- Place an object like a bandanna, marker flag, or blaze on a tree or trail as a symbolic rescue signal. Let it serve as a visual reminder that God sees you.
- Challenge yourself to write a short prayer of full surrender—then say it out loud under the open sky.

WILD TANGLE

Most survival instructors rarely mention their mistakes, let alone feature them. There's a fear, I suppose, that if we reveal the times we've failed, people might doubt our knowledge or question our credibility. But the truth is that every skilled outdoorsman has learned more from their failures than their successes. I know I have. In fact, some of my greatest teachers in life have been my worst mistakes.

I'll never forget teaching a survival course several years ago. It was one of those crisp, golden fall days. I was leading the wild edible plants portion of the course, excited to show the group how to find and eat nutritious plants in the wild. I spotted a wild burdock plant, a great find. The root of burdock is edible and rich in nutrients. In fact, it is a cultivated crop in some regions of the world. I couldn't wait to demonstrate.

I knelt down, dug into the earth, and pulled out the burdock root. Twisted around it was another root, which I didn't recognize. I cast it aside without much thought, cleaned the dirt off the burdock root, and took a few hearty bites in front of the group to show that it was safe.

The course wrapped up. Everyone left. But not long after, I started to feel sick. It came on fast in the form of nausea, dizziness, and disorientation. My stomach turned violently. Then came uncontrollable vomiting. I could barely stand. I knew something was seriously wrong.

I returned to the spot where I had dug up the root and took a closer look. That's when it hit me. The root I'd tossed aside—that was the burdock root. The one I'd eaten was pokeweed.

All of my wild edible plant field manuals told me that eating pokeweed root can be fatal.

During the digging process, the green leaves I had used to identify the burdock plant became separated from the root. The tangled pokeweed root looked very similar to burdock. I'll never forget the lesson: Never eat a root that isn't still connected to the leaves you used to identify it.

Within minutes, I was in the ER, slipping in and out of consciousness. For twenty-four hours, I lay in a hospital bed, uncertain if I'd walk out alive. All because of a tangle of roots and a moment of misplaced confidence.

This was one of the most humbling moments of my entire survival career. But later, as I began to take my walk with Jesus more seriously, I couldn't shake the spiritual parallels between that experience and my life as a believer.

Life, I've learned, is a lot like that wild edible plants course. It's easy to get comfortable. It's easy to get complacent. And that's exactly when the enemy makes his move. First Peter 5:8 warns us to "be alert and of sober mind. Your enemy the devil prowls around like a roaring lion looking for someone to devour."

Satan doesn't always come charging in with something obviously evil. Sometimes he masquerades as something good, something helpful, something beautiful, or something harmless. Second Corinthians 11:14 speaks to Satan's annoying habit of doing this: "And no wonder, for Satan himself masquerades as an angel of light."

That day, I mistook something deadly for something nourishing, and it almost cost me everything. The same thing can happen in our spiritual lives. The enemy tangles toxic things around our hearts, such as bad habits, unhealthy relationships, false idols, and distractions that pull our focus from what matters most.

Often, the danger grows not because we're defiant but because we're distracted, tired, prideful, or trying to impress others. We start putting on a show instead of walking in truth. First Corinthians 10:12 warns us to be careful: "So, if you think you are standing firm, be careful that you don't fall!"

Behind the scenes, we stop examining the root and stop testing the fruit. And we begin to consume what looks good on the surface but is filled with poison underneath.

Even good things like a job, a romantic relationship, or a talent can become dangerous when tangled with the wrong motivations. The devil doesn't always need to attack with what's evil; sometimes he simply twists what's good. Proverbs 1:32 reminds us to not be complacent, as "the complacency of fools will destroy them."

It's not always the plant that's the problem. Sometimes it's what's tangled around it.

IN THE WILD

Verses to Contemplate

The kingdom of heaven is like a man who sowed good seed in his field. But while everyone was sleeping, his enemy came and sowed weeds among the wheat, and went away. (Matt. 13:24–25)

QUESTIONS FOR THE WILDERNESS JOURNAL

1. Can you identify something in your life that looks good on the surface but may be tangled with something harmful right alongside it?
2. Where have you grown complacent in your walk with Jesus—trusting your own strength or experience more than His guidance?
3. What roots do you need to examine more closely in this season of your life?

PRAYER OF THE DAY

Father, forgive me for the times I've let my guard down. Forgive me for my pride, my distractions, and my spiritual laziness. Help me stay alert. Teach me to examine the roots of the things I consume spiritually, emotionally, and physically. I want to walk in truth, not assumption. Guard my heart from the tangles of the enemy, even when they come disguised as good things. Thank You for turning even my failures into lessons that bring me closer to You. In Jesus's name, amen.

WILDERNESS APPLICATION

Go for a walk in the woods or in your backyard. Look for a plant or tree with tangled vines or other growth around it. Sit near it and reflect on these questions:

- What good thing in my life might be getting choked out by something else?
- Where do I need to untangle pride, distraction, or spiritual laziness?

Write down one area of your life this week where you will practice greater diligence and discernment.

WILD ORDER

I'll never forget taking a hike in one of the most unique geological areas in the world: Red River Gorge, located in eastern Kentucky. My best friend Justin and I were in high school and had pulled away from our normal routine for the thrill of adventure.

Red River Gorge is known for its towering sandstone cliffs, massive rock faces, hidden rock shelters, and incredible natural stone arches carved by the great flood in the time of Noah. It's a place where steep walls rise hundreds of feet, and narrow trails twist and wind through rugged terrain that feels wild and untouched. For two teenagers, it was a land of adventure and freedom.

While hiking off-trail and looking for a spot to camp, we rappelled down a large cliff and plunged into areas that seemed to us like they had never been seen by human eyes before. We felt like we were exploring new lands for the very first time.

As we skirted along the base of a steep limestone cliff, we turned a corner, and it opened up into a large, recessed area that had been carved out by hundreds of years of erosion. But what we found literally shook us to the core.

Built up against and underneath this outcropping was a stone dwelling with walls stacked neatly from floor to ceiling, forming the exterior wall of a crude cave dwelling. Our first response was natural: "I wonder who made this."

Any human on earth, if they had turned that corner with us, would have asked the same question. What civilization, at what point in history, stacked these rocks and built this cave dwelling? Not for one second would anyone have looked upon this structure in the middle of the wilderness and thought it was created by random chance or by any act other than the engineering mind of another human.

I think about this moment often, how quickly we gave credit to early humans for this structure, and that it was nothing more than neatly stacked rocks. These rocks weren't interacting with one another. They weren't forming any type of live, functional system. They were just simply piled on top of one another to form what was clearly an exterior wall of a cave dwelling. At the end of the day, they were just rocks stacked in an order that clearly pointed to a human creator.

I also often think about how there's not a single person on the planet who would argue with me that those stacked rocks were designed and built for a purpose and their order had a designer.

And this is why I am baffled at how so many people can look at things on this earth that are infinitely more complex, infinitely more engineered and ordered, and not credit a Creator, a Designer, or an Engineer. They chalk even the most complex of organisms up to random happenstance at some point in history or to a primordial soup of some sort.

Even the simplest bacteria have more order than that cliff dwelling could ever have. Even a fly on a pile of rhino dung has infinitely more engineering and design than those stacked stones. A flower is incomprehensibly more complex. And the systems within the human body that allow us to operate, think, digest, react, repair, and even build cliff dwellings are unfathomably more ordered than that stone wall in the Kentucky wilderness.

How can someone possibly credit a stack of rocks to a creator, but not credit the miracles of creation to the Mastermind Creator who not only has infinite creativity but infinite knowledge and capability?

Scientists and engineers have been trying for millennia to recreate some of the most basic things in nature, such as a spider web, which a spider instinctively spins from its abdomen by mixing proteins in milliseconds. Yet even our smartest minds can't fully recreate its strength, stretch, and lightness.

And if that example isn't enough, consider the human blood-clotting system. When you get a cut, your body triggers over twenty separate chemical steps in perfect sequence, each dependent on the last, to stop the bleeding. If even one step is missing, you bleed to death. If one step happens too soon, you can die from a clot. It's an all-or-nothing system. There is no halfway version. It's impossible for such a system to develop "little by little." It works only as a complete, perfectly functioning design, right from the start.

The Designer of our systems, and our world, and our galaxies, and our bacteria, and our animals, and our flowers, and our human bodies is incomprehensible. And that in itself is the explanation. It's so complicated, so perfectly ordered, that it is beyond human comprehension, and for some, that makes it easier to deny Him than to admit the truth.

The Bible, of course, sets the record straight. It gives credit where credit is due. Romans 1:20 clearly states, "For since the creation of the world God's invisible qualities—his eternal power and divine nature—have been clearly seen, being understood from what has been made, so that people are without excuse."

The same way no one would deny that a cliff dwelling had a builder, creation itself testifies to God's design, and we are without excuse for ignoring the evidence. Colossians 1:16–17 confidently proclaims that "in him all things were created: things in heaven and on earth, visible and invisible . . . all things have been created through him and for him. He is before all things, and in him all things hold together."

Every intricate system, from galaxies to the clotting of your blood, is held together by Christ. It's all from Him and for Him. Without Him, the order collapses. Psalm 19:1–4 reminds us that creation is God's silent preacher. It never stops proclaiming His handiwork: "The heavens declare the glory of God; the skies proclaim the work of his hands. . . . Their voice goes out into all the earth, their words to the ends of the world" (vv. 1, 4).

In Job 38:4–7, God Himself reminds us that creation didn't happen by accident. It was measured, planned, and executed with purpose: "Where were you when I laid the earth's foundation? Tell me, if you understand. Who marked off its dimensions? Surely you know!" (vv. 4–5).

The incomprehensible order in creation should never be an excuse to deny God's design; rather, it stands as overwhelming proof that there must be a Designer.

IN THE WILD

Verse to Contemplate

For since the creation of the world God's invisible qualities—his eternal power and divine nature—have been clearly seen, being understood from what has been made, so that people are without excuse. (Rom. 1:20)

QUESTIONS FOR THE WILDERNESS JOURNAL

1. Have you ever overlooked God's handiwork in the everyday details of life?
2. What's one part of creation that recently reminded you of His order and design?
3. How does recognizing God as the Designer affect your faith and trust in Him?
4. What would change in your daily life if you gave Him credit for every detail, from the smallest breath to the largest galaxy?

PRAYER OF THE DAY

Lord, open my eyes to see Your hand in all of creation. Help me give You glory for the beauty, order, and design around me. Forgive me for the times I've overlooked Your craftsmanship, taken it for granted, or chalked it up to chance. Teach me to live in awe of You, the Master Creator, and to continually give credit where it is due. In Jesus's name, amen.

WILDERNESS APPLICATION

- Go outside and identify three examples of design in nature—a leaf, a bird, or even the clouds. Pause and thank God for each.
- Sketch or photograph a natural pattern (like tree rings or spider webs) and write how it points you back to God's creativity.
- Try building something simple outdoors (e.g., stacking stones into a small cairn) and reflect on how much more order God has built into living systems.
- On your next hike, stop at a viewpoint and spend five minutes in silence, letting creation preach to you about its Creator.

WILD HURRY

A few years ago, I taught a bow drill class to a group of young, successful executives. The bow drill is a classic survival fire starting method that uses a string and bow to spin a wooden spindle into a hearth board, creating friction, heat, and ultimately an ember. They were smart, fit, eager, and ready to tackle a new skill. We spent nearly two hours carefully carving perfect bow drill kits together, and I shared all my secrets for success. I made sure each person had the right materials and techniques to succeed at making fire.

But when it came time to light that first spark, the race was on. Excitement and nerves took over, and they rushed the process. Suddenly, my perfectly prepared students found themselves with broken spindles, crushed hearth boards, and growing frustration.

All they had to do was stay calm, listen, and follow my proven advice. It was a simple process, yet incredibly challenging in the midst of how the world wires us to think.

This is more than a lesson for my survival classes; it's a reality for all of us. In survival situations, rushing almost always leads to failure, especially when making fire!

Yet, even with years of understanding this truth in the wilderness, I spent a good part of my life hurrying through everything else. I thought that being "productive" was the goal, and I took pride in filling my days with busyness.

But then a friend shared a quote that's often attributed to Corrie ten Boom, the author of *The Hiding Place*: "If the devil can't make you bad, he'll make you busy."

The more we fill our time with meaningless distractions, the more distant we become from what really matters. I realized I was like those bow drill students, rushing through life, focused on productivity but losing sight of the real important end goal.

There is a cost to endless rushing and striving. Looking back, I see how my own life was like the proverbial frog in boiling water: As the water heats up slowly, the frog doesn't realize the danger until it's too late. Surrounded by worldly goals and a bunch of even more meaningless busyness, like social media, I hadn't noticed how far I'd drifted from my relationship with Jesus. Like that frog, I was in the water, surrounded by things that didn't matter, unaware of the cost. I was too busy for prayer, too busy to read God's truth, and too busy to spend time in solitude with Him.

God's plan for us is simple: to love Him with all our heart, mind, and soul. We become the best version of ourselves when we honor Him in everything we do.

The rewards of this are detailed in Psalm 23: "He makes me lie down in green pastures, he leads me beside quiet waters, he refreshes my soul. He guides me along the right paths for his name's sake" (vv. 2–3).

Over the past few years, I've made a commitment to spend time with Jesus through solitude in nature, Scripture study, and prayer. The more I get to know Jesus, the more I want to know Jesus.

I've learned that anchoring each day in Philippians 4:6–7 gives the peace and purpose that all my past busyness ruthlessly stripped away: "Do not be anxious about anything, but in every situation, by prayer and petition, with thanksgiving, present your requests to God. And the peace of God, which transcends all understanding, will guard your hearts and your minds in Christ Jesus."

Busyness is physically, emotionally, and spiritually exhausting. But Jesus offers a reprieve from that exhaustion in Matthew 11:28, saying, "Come to me, all you who are weary and burdened, and I will give you rest."

I can tell you firsthand that rest is real. In my own life, I've stopped trying to create my own identity through doing and have instead sought rest in my true identity as a child of God.

Maybe this resonates with you. Are you caught up in more of the temporal than the eternal these days?

Are you, like me and my students with the bow drill, rushing through life and missing the peace that comes from following His pace?

I've had my fair share of sins, and "being busy" is definitely one of the ways the devil kept my priorities out of whack. Let the Scriptures in today's devotional be powerful reminders of the toll that hurry can take on our lives, especially when it keeps us from becoming the best versions of ourselves that God intended.

IN THE WILD

Verse to Contemplate

Come to me, all you who are weary and burdened, and I will give you rest. (Matt. 11:28)

QUESTIONS FOR THE WILDERNESS JOURNAL

1. In what areas of your life are you rushing instead of resting?
2. What "false fires" of busyness have distracted you from hearing God's voice clearly?
3. When was the last time you slowed down long enough to simply be with Jesus?
4. What does meaningful rest look like for you, and how can you pursue it more intentionally this week?
5. What might God be trying to say to you in stillness that you've been too busy to hear?

PRAYER OF THE DAY

Jesus, I'm tired of rushing. I've spent too much time chasing the wrong things and filling my life with distractions. Teach me to slow down. Lead me beside Your quiet waters. Help me trade performance for presence and busyness for true rest. I want to walk at Your pace and live from the peace You offer. Thank You for always waiting for me, even when I'm running too fast to notice. In Your name I pray, amen.

WILDERNESS APPLICATION

- Spend time outside without a phone or agenda. Sit beside a creek, under a tree, or on a patch of grass, and simply rest in God's presence.
- Practice a wilderness Sabbath. Take a few hours to be alone with God in nature and ask Him to reset your priorities.
- Try making fire by friction (e.g., using a bow drill). Pay attention to how patience, rhythm, and restraint are more effective than force.
- Sketch a picture of your "quiet waters" during your next wilderness quiet time.
- Remove one thing from your schedule this week that drains you and doesn't align with God's priorities for your life. Replace it with a short hike in creation.

WILD PREPAREDNESS

In addition to teaching wilderness survival skills, I also spend a good deal of my time teaching, writing about, and providing expert commentary on disaster preparedness. This includes not only how to survive any number of natural or man-made disasters, but more importantly, how to prepare for them in advance. That preparation ranges from building a seventy-two-hour bug out bag and purifying water at home to long-term food storage and sustainable living.

One of the most popular preparedness topics I teach is long-term food storage. It covers a wide range of strategies: stocking up on freeze-dried foods, growing your own garden, keeping livestock, canning, dehydrating, home freeze-drying, and storing up bulk goods in case the food supply chain is disrupted. My books *The Disaster-Ready Home* and *Disaster Survival 101* focus specifically on these topics and more. For many, long-term food storage can sound very overwhelming, and it can be. So, I encourage people to start with something simple: a system called rotation.

Rotation is the idea of choosing the top ten items your family regularly eats that have a long shelf life and simply buying a few more of them each time you go to the store. Items like pasta, rice, oatmeal, peanut butter, boxed mixes, or canned goods are good choices. These are things that won't spoil quickly and are used often. Over time, this creates a reliable backstock of daily-use foods, without a huge upfront investment or change in eating habits.

In the event of a disaster, rotation allows you to fall back on what you already know. You're not eating strange new meals or learning new systems under pressure. You've already built the discipline of preparedness into your daily life. With this back-stock of rotation food, you know how to use it, how to prepare it, and what to expect.

The key is that you don't panic. Instead, you pivot.

Just like natural disasters, such as tornadoes, hurricanes, and power outages, unexpected spiritual disasters can strike too. These can take the form of a tragedy, a temptation, a slow drift into lukewarmness, a subtle lie from the enemy, or an attack when your guard is down.

And if we haven't prepared our hearts in advance, we won't know how to respond when those storms come. We'll be scrambling, unsure, and reactive at a time when what we need is spiritual readiness. First Peter 5:8 warns us, "Be alert and of sober mind. Your enemy the devil prowls around like a roaring lion looking for someone to devour." That's not a verse about paranoia but about preparation. It's not fearmongering, it's readiness training. And the kind of spiritual readiness that withstands temptation, anxiety, grief, spiritual burnout, and false teachings doesn't come from a last-minute cram session. It comes from what respected theologian Dallas Willard called "indirect preparedness." Indirect preparedness is the discipline in the background of your life that quietly equips you to respond appropriately when the unexpected hits.

Just like food storage rotation builds physical preparedness, spiritual rotation builds spiritual preparedness. These rotation rhythms take the form of

- daily Scripture reading,
- daily prayer,
- daily solitude with the Lord,
- daily community with other believers,
- daily confession and realignment, and
- daily worship and thanksgiving.

These disciplines may seem small at the time, but like buying backstock of food items on each trip to the grocery store, they accumulate. They build spiritual muscle memory. They give you something to draw from when crisis strikes.

Instead of panicking, you pray. You pivot toward the Lord, because you've trained, through daily spiritual rotation, to do just that. Psalm 119:11 reminds us of this concept: "I have hidden your word in my heart that I might not sin against you."

Instead of food for the body, we store up truth for the soul. Hebrews 5:14 says that this training can help us discern good from evil: "Solid food is for the mature, who by constant use have trained themselves to distinguish good from evil."

Daily intake of Scripture is how we're equipped. We practice now so that we can stand firm later, just as 2 Timothy 3:16–17 says: "All Scripture is God-breathed and is useful for teaching, rebuking, correcting and training in righteousness, so that the servant of God may be thoroughly equipped for every good work."

All the physical preparedness in the world means nothing if you aren't spiritually prepared for what comes next. And this comes from someone who teaches physical preparedness for a living. Are you ready to build your own system of spiritual rotation? Begin with one of these disciplines: prayer, Bible reading, or solitude. Let it become part of your daily lifestyle. You don't have to master it all today. Just start small. Stock the shelves of your heart with truth and restock them regularly.

And when the spiritual storm comes, you'll not just survive but thrive.

IN THE WILD

Verses to Contemplate

> Train yourself to be godly. For physical training is of some value, but godliness has value for all things, holding promise for both the present life and the life to come. (1 Tim. 4:7–8)

QUESTIONS FOR THE WILDERNESS JOURNAL

1. What spiritual discipline do you tend to neglect but know you need in order to be prepared?

2. Are you spiritually preparing daily, or only reacting when storms hit?
3. What's one way you can build more spiritual rotation into your normal routine this week?
4. When the last spiritual disaster struck, how did you respond? What could you learn from that?
5. What small action can you take today to begin training in godliness?

PRAYER OF THE DAY

God, I want to be spiritually prepared, not just for emergencies but for everyday faithfulness. Teach me to stock my heart with Your Word, to rotate Your truth into my daily life, and to train my spirit with disciplines that draw me close to You. Build in me a rhythm of readiness so that I'm anchored when the storms of life come. In Jesus's name, amen.

WILDERNESS APPLICATION

- Just like inspecting your bug out bag, take inventory of your spiritual life. What's missing? What's expired? What needs restocking?
- Write down five spiritual disciplines (e.g., Bible reading, prayer, silence, community, worship, solitude, service). Choose one each day this week and commit to doing it. Small actions lead to lasting transformation.

- Memorize one verse this week that prepares your heart for hardship (try Psalm 119:11 or Matthew 7:24). Write it down and post it somewhere visible, such as your dashboard, mirror, or wallet.
- Go for a walk or run and reflect on this idea: If physical training prepares you for wilderness survival, what does spiritual training prepare you for? Let that connection motivate consistency.
- Simulate a spiritual crisis. Journal or talk through what your first response would be. Then plan your pivot: What truth or discipline will you lean on when the storm comes?

WILD QUICKSAND

Not long ago, I filmed an episode of *Could You Survive? with Creek Stewart* that focused on the true story of a couple who went on what was supposed to be a simple day hike through a canyon trail in Utah. The trail hugged a swollen creek still recovering from recent rains. The water wasn't high enough to close the trail, but the ground had been saturated for days.

Several miles in, the boyfriend went to cross a sandy patch of the creek to get to the other side. But as soon as he stepped into it, he sank to his knees in what turned out to be quicksand. In just minutes, his legs were buried up to his thighs. He and his girlfriend tried everything they could to free him, but it only made things worse. The more he fought it, the deeper he sank.

Eventually, his girlfriend had to leave him behind in the near-freezing water to find help. Nightfall was closing in, temperatures were dropping, and things were looking grim. Thankfully, she reached rescuers just in time, and a specialized team was able to save him. The rescue process involved a pulley system to loosen the soil around his legs because, by that point, extraction by strength alone was impossible.

Here's what I've learned: The worst thing you can do in quicksand is panic. The more you thrash and fight, the faster you sink. You've got to calm your breathing, minimize movement, and accept that rescue, not self-reliance, is your only hope.

That survival reality is deeply spiritual too.

I imagine that's exactly how Peter felt when he stepped out of the boat to meet Jesus on the water. For a few miraculous steps, Peter walked across the surface of the sea, defying nature. But then he looked around. The waves were high. The wind was loud. His confidence turned to fear, and he began to sink. Matthew 14:29–31 tells us the full story:

> Then Peter got down out of the boat, walked on the water and came toward Jesus. But when he saw the wind, he was afraid and, beginning to sink, cried out, "Lord, save me!"
>
> Immediately Jesus reached out his hand and caught him. "You of little faith," he said, "why did you doubt?"

Sometimes life can feel like we're sinking in deep water or stuck in quicksand. Grief can be overwhelming. Anxiety can grip us from depths that are hard to understand. Sin and addiction can have a quicksand-like hold on our soul. Loneliness can feel like uncontrollable waves around us. When we feel ourselves sinking in life, our first instinct is to panic. We try to fix it. We flail, isolate, overthink, get angry, and fall into despair. But just like in real quicksand, panic only pulls us deeper.

There are moments in life when we realize we can't get out of this on our own. That's when we must do what Peter did above.

We need to cry out to and reach for Jesus. Psalm 69:1–2 says it this way: "Save me, O God, for the waters have come up to my neck. I sink in the miry depths, where there is no foothold."

Sometimes life doesn't feel like a storm. It feels like mud that is silent, slow, and suffocating. There's no thunder, just silence. No waves, just weight. That's what depression, anxiety, fear, addiction, sin, and grief can feel like. It's like you're being swallowed slowly, and no one sees it. But Jesus sees it. He's not just watching from a distance. He's reaching out a hand to keep your head above water: "When you pass through the waters, I will be with you; and when you pass through the rivers, they will not sweep over you" (Isa. 43:2).

He doesn't promise you'll never find yourself sinking. But He does promise you'll never be alone. When you feel overwhelmed and buried by life's weight, His hand is near. He's not frustrated. He's not ashamed of you. He's not afraid to get dirty. He's the Rescuer, and He's waiting for you to reach out, just like Peter did. Hebrews 12:2 calls us to fix "our eyes on Jesus, the pioneer and perfecter of faith." The storm didn't stop when Peter stepped out of the boat. And it didn't stop when he started sinking. But something changed when he stopped looking at the storm and started looking at Jesus. His eyes refocused.

If you're stuck in a storm or spiritual quicksand right now, it's time to look up. Fix your eyes on Jesus again. Call His name. Stop struggling in your own strength. He is already reaching out. He'll do the same for you as in Psalm 40:2: "He lifted me out of the slimy pit, out of the mud and mire; he set my feet on a rock and gave me a firm place to stand."

What a promise. Jesus doesn't just pull us out, He sets us on solid ground. He puts us back on our feet and gives us a new path forward. And John 14:27 reminds us to not be afraid, as Jesus says, "Peace I leave with you; my peace I give you. . . . Do not let your hearts be troubled and do not be afraid."

Peace doesn't always mean immediate escape from the storm or the mud. Sometimes it's the calm assurance that you've been seen, heard, and held by the One who never sinks.

IN THE WILD

Verse to Contemplate

> He lifted me out of the slimy pit, out of the mud and mire; he set my feet on a rock and gave me a firm place to stand. (Ps. 40:2)

QUESTIONS FOR THE WILDERNESS JOURNAL

1. Have you ever felt like you were emotionally or spiritually stuck in quicksand? What caused it?
2. What's been your first reaction in those moments? Panic, pride, or prayer?
3. In what area of your life do you need to stop struggling and reach out to Jesus?
4. Where might God be calling you to refocus your eyes on Him?
5. Who in your life might be silently sinking right now, and how can you reach out and offer the peace of Christ?

PRAYER OF THE DAY

Lord Jesus, I feel the weight of the world sometimes, like I'm sinking in mud I can't get free from. I confess that I often try to fix things on my own, but it only pulls me deeper. I need You. Reach out and take hold of me. Set my feet on solid ground. Calm my heart and fill me with Your peace. I choose to fix my eyes on You again. I trust You to be my Rescuer and my Rock. In Your name, amen.

WILDERNESS APPLICATION

- Go to a creek or muddy area and carefully press your foot into soft ground. Reflect on how difficult it would be to escape if you were truly stuck. Imagine the peace it would bring to know someone is coming to help.
- Write a letter to Jesus from the quicksand of your current situation. Be honest. Then write His response to you based on the Scriptures above.
- On one side of a piece of paper, write "Peter Sinking." On the other side, write "Jesus Reaching." On Peter's side, write what you're currently overwhelmed by. On Jesus's side, write words of hope and rescue.
- Set a timer for five minutes and sit outside in silence with your eyes closed. Repeat this prayer: "Lord, help me not panic. Help me fix my eyes on You."

WILD THORNS

One of my favorite survival skills is improvised fishing. When you're out in the wild without the luxury of a tackle box, you begin to realize just how spoiled we are in modern society with barbed metal fishing hooks. For generations, Indigenous cultures used natural materials to craft effective fishing tools, such as abraded slate hooks, sharpened bone gorges, and carved antler tips. Their resourcefulness was mind-boggling and inspiring.

One natural hook I've used with success is almost ready-made: the large curved, barbed thorn of the wild rose.

Wild rose thorns are talon-like. They are curved, razor-sharp, and surprisingly strong. When you cut a section of rose branch that includes one, two, or even three thorns all facing in the same direction, it can become a primitive fishing hook. Bait is tied onto the shaft, unlike threading it on a modern hook. But because rose thorns lack a barb to keep the fish from shaking free, the fishing method changes. You fish for small panfish and pull them quickly from the water before they can wiggle loose. It's not unlike the method used in tuna pole fishing where you hook fast, yank fast, land fast.

Rose thorn fishing isn't the most effective method, but it works. And in a survival situation, that's all that matters. In many areas of the world, rose thorns are abundant, free, and available year-round to the resourceful wilderness survivor.

There are other abundant thorns in our life as well. Paul describes thorns in the flesh in 2 Corinthians 12. He talks about a thorn of his own, but his thorn had nothing to do with fishing.

> Therefore, in order to keep me from becoming conceited, I was given a thorn in my flesh, a messenger of Satan, to torment me. Three times I pleaded with the Lord to take it away from me. But he said to me, "My grace is sufficient for you, for my power is made perfect in weakness." Therefore I will boast all the more gladly about my weaknesses, so that Christ's power may rest on me. That is why, for Christ's sake, I delight in weaknesses, in insults, in hardships, in persecutions, in difficulties. For when I am weak, then I am strong. (vv. 7–10)

Paul's thorn was never defined. It might have been a physical ailment, a spiritual battle, or a persistent hardship. It could have even been guilt from his days of persecuting Christ followers. All we know is that it was painful, humbling, and chronic. He passionately begged God to remove it three times, and God said no.

Instead, God offered him something unexpected: "My grace is sufficient for you" (v. 9). Instead of a healing, God gives Paul grace.

If I'm honest, I've wrestled with that answer. What does that mean? How can God's grace replace healing? How can His power be "made perfect" in the very place I feel weakest?

I don't have all the answers, but I know this: Paul isn't the only one who's lived with a thorn. I have too. And chances are, you're living with one as well.

At ten years old, a small dry, scaly patch of skin appeared on my leg. Soon after, I was diagnosed with psoriasis, a chronic skin condition that causes painful, inflamed, and very visible patches on the body. It showed up at one of the most vulnerable and formative times in my life, and it's stayed with me ever since.

I constantly prayed for it to go away. I asked God to heal me in middle school, so kids wouldn't make fun of my dandruff. I asked Him in gym class, so I wouldn't have anxiety over playing shirts versus skins. I asked in high school, in college, and when I started dating my wife. I asked Him again before my first television show, praying I wouldn't have to strip down for any survival scenes. And I asked again when each of my three children were born, hoping they wouldn't inherit it.

But like Paul, no matter how many times I asked, the thorn remained. God has said no for over thirty years. I've learned that God isn't ignoring my prayers but that He's purposefully not answering them. And by doing so, He is offering something deeper than a healing. This concept is very difficult to explain.

While I've learned to manage my psoriasis better now through diet and lifestyle, it has never fully left. It flares when I'm stressed. It humbles me when I'm feeling proud. It reminds me that I'm not in control.

Here's the mystery of the thorn I want to share with you: Even though the thorn has stayed, so has God. It's hard to imagine there might be something better in store for us than miraculous healing. But God's ways are bigger than our ways. It's in the middle of my struggle that I've encountered His grace, not just as a comforting idea but as a real, sustaining force in my life. And what's crazy is that my psoriasis has actually deepened my faith and reliance on the Lord. I've learned that persistent thorns have a unique way of doing this in several different ways.

First, thorns keep us close to God. Psoriasis has been a lifelong reason for me to pray. I've likely prayed over my psoriasis more than any other thing in my life. It's cultivated a habit of going to God first, not as a last resort. I have been in constant communication with the Lord over the years because of my psoriasis.

Second, thorns help us build compassion for others. My thorn has helped me become more empathetic and less judgmental toward other people who struggle with health issues, especially skin conditions. I see pain differently now. I understand hidden battles. Grace has turned pain into tenderness, and it's opened the door for conversation, and even ministry, on more than one occasion.

Third, thorns can keep pride at bay and encourage humility. In a world obsessed with image, psoriasis has forced me to root my identity in something deeper. I've learned I'm not defined by my skin, my image, or people's approval. Instead, I am defined by who God says I am.

Fourth, thorns teach us where true strength comes from. I used to believe that I had to be strong—and perfect—for God to use me. But psoriasis has taught me otherwise. God's power shows up best in the places I can't control or fix.

And last, thorns keep us longing for God's promise of eternity. Living with something unhealed makes you long for heaven more. The thorn makes me ache for the day when everything broken will be made whole. That longing, too, is grace and hope all combined into one hard-to-define emotion.

Maybe you, too, are living with a chronic illness, a mental health struggle, a long-term grief, or invisible wounds. If so, there just might be something more powerful, more meaningful, and more impactful for you to experience here on earth because of your thorn that you would not experience if God gave you an instant healing.

Healings may deliver, but they do not develop relationship with God and dependence on Him like thorns do.

IN THE WILD

Verse to Contemplate

> But he said to me, "My grace is sufficient for you, for my power is made perfect in weakness." Therefore I will boast all the more gladly about my weaknesses, so that Christ's power may rest on me. (2 Cor. 12:9)

QUESTIONS FOR THE WILDERNESS JOURNAL

1. What is the thorn in your life that you've asked God to remove?
2. Can you recall a time when God met you with grace in the middle of that struggle?
3. How has your thorn shaped your character, compassion, or dependence on God?

4. In what area of weakness might God be showing His strength through you right now?
5. Have you allowed your thorn to push you toward God—or away from Him?

PRAYER OF THE DAY

Lord, I don't always like the thorn You've allowed in my life. It humbles me, hurts me, and reminds me of my limitations. But I trust that Your grace is enough. Even when I feel weak, You are strong. Teach me to see my thorn as an invitation to deeper dependence. Help me rest in Your presence and rely on Your strength. Let this weakness become a place of worship, where Your power can be seen and my faith can be increased. In Jesus's name, amen.

WILDERNESS APPLICATION

Find a thorny plant such as a wild rose, blackberry, or even a thistle while on a hike or outdoor walk. Pause to examine it up close. Notice its beauty and its danger. Sketch or journal about it. As you reflect, name your personal thorn aloud to God. Instead of asking Him to remove it today, ask Him to reveal His grace through it. Ask Him to use it to increase your faith. Carry a small thorn or sketch of one with you this week as a tangible reminder that He may not take it away, but He will never leave you in it alone.

WILD TREES

Trees have been a very big part of my life and career as a survival instructor. Honestly, if it weren't for trees, I wouldn't be in business. Almost every aspect of my wilderness survival training business involves a tree or a tree part of some sort.

I use trees to teach shelter building, knife and axe skills, trap making, basketmaking, campcraft, cordage skills, fire making, cooking, spear making, wild edible identification, and the list goes on forever. From the moment a survival course begins, my students and I are working with trees.

Let's just take the eastern white pine, for example.

Did you know pine resin is highly flammable and can be used in fire building? Fatwood, also known as pitchwood, is pine wood saturated in pine resin, and it's one of the best fire starters on earth. Pine resin is also antibacterial and can be used to seal cuts and scrapes (just like how the tree uses it). Pine resin can also be used to make a natural epoxy when mixed with charcoal. This can be used to waterproof containers made from the flexible bark of the same tree. Pine needles can be steeped in water to make a tea rich in vitamin C. They also make fantastic fire tinder, bedding material, roofing material, and insulation. The inner bark of the pine tree is even edible and can also be used as improvised cordage. Sheets of pine bark can be formed into various containers, and pine nuts are edible and can also be used as bait.

Eastern white pine trees are amazing, and that's just one tree in a global forest of over seventy thousand different species of trees! God hardwired an infinite array of survival resources for us into the plants and trees of creation. Not only have I developed a great respect for trees as a survival instructor, but as a student of creation I've developed a reverence for them as well.

The more I read the Bible, the more I realize that God loves trees too. A lot. Genesis 1:11–13 tells us that trees are actually the first living thing God made on earth, even before humans: "Then God said, 'Let the land produce vegetation: seed-bearing plants and trees on the land that bear fruit with seed in it, according to their various kinds.' And it was so. The land produced vegetation: plants bearing seed according to their kinds and trees bearing fruit with seed in it according to their kinds. And God saw that it was good. And there was evening, and there was morning—the third day."

Trees are mentioned everywhere in the Bible, from beginning to end. Take Genesis 2:8–9, for example: "Now the Lord God had planted a garden in the east, in Eden; and there he put the man he had formed. The Lord God made all kinds of trees grow out of the ground—trees that were pleasing to the eye and good for food. In the middle of the garden were the tree of life and the tree of the knowledge of good and evil."

Literally one of the first conversations God has with Adam is about trees: "The Lord God took the man and put him in the Garden of Eden to work it and take care of it. And the Lord God commanded the man, 'You are free to eat from any tree in the garden; but you must not eat from the tree of the knowledge of good and evil, for when you eat from it you will certainly die'" (vv. 15–17).

Without a doubt, the most meaningful event in the Bible involving a tree and saving people is when Jesus Himself, who was also a carpenter, hung on a wooden cross to die for the sins of the world. In the end, it is just Jesus and a tree that changed the course of history.

There is also a very encouraging tree reference in Jeremiah 17:5–8:

> This is what the Lord says:
>
> "Cursed is the one who trusts in man,
> who draws strength from mere flesh
> and whose heart turns away from the Lord.
> That person will be like a bush in the wastelands;
> they will not see prosperity when it comes.
> They will dwell in the parched places of the desert,
> in a salt land where no one lives.
> But blessed is the one who trusts in the Lord,
> whose confidence is in him.
> They will be like a tree planted by the water
> that sends out its roots by the stream.
> It does not fear when heat comes;
> its leaves are always green.
> It has no worries in a year of drought
> and never fails to bear fruit."

Roots by the stream, leaves always green, and never failing to bear fruit. To be this kind of tree we must remain in and trust in Him.

And here's something that didn't happen at random. The bronchi of our lungs look exactly like trees. In fact, the Cleveland Clinic describes them in this exact way: "Your bronchi are part of the tracheobronchial tree, which includes your trachea, bronchi and bronchioles. Your tracheobronchial tree looks like an upside-down tree with the trachea as the trunk and the bronchi representing the branches."[1]

Not only do our bronchi look like trees, these treelike structures are critical to our survival. They assist in processing the oxygen we breathe in order to stay alive. The oxygen converts to carbon dioxide, which we exhale. But guess where the oxygen comes from? You guessed it—trees. Trees produce oxygen through a process called photosynthesis, where they absorb carbon dioxide (that we produce with the help of our treelike bronchi), use sunlight as energy, and combine it with water to create oxygen as a byproduct while also producing food for the tree in the form of sugar. Essentially, they "breathe in" carbon dioxide and "breathe out" oxygen. God created trees first because we depend on them for survival.

It's easy to take the complexity and marvelousness of creation for granted. Nothing about it is random; it is all interconnected and woven together by the same Designer. I believe that marveling at creation is a form of worship. Standing in awe before and amid it shows reverence to the Creator. Intentionally thanking

1. "Bronchi," Cleveland Clinic, updated May 5, 2025, http://my.clevelandclinic.org/health/body/21607-bronchi.

God for the indescribably complex and miraculously engineered things in nature around us, like trees, is without question a form of praise. It's important to take time out of our busy lives to praise the Creator for the awesome things in nature He has allowed us to observe and interact with. His creativity is unrivaled, and His desire is for us to marvel at it! But worship is always reserved for the Creator, not creation. Admire the creation but worship the Creator.

If you loved this discussion about trees, consider picking up *Reforesting Faith* by my friend Dr. Matthew Sleeth, which takes a deep dive into the trees of the Bible.

IN THE WILD

Verse to Contemplate

They will be like a tree planted by the water
  that sends out its roots by the stream.
It does not fear when heat comes;
  its leaves are always green.
It has no worries in a year of drought
  and never fails to bear fruit. (Jer. 17:8)

QUESTIONS FOR THE WILDERNESS JOURNAL

1. In what ways do you see God using trees in your life, both literally and symbolically?
2. What does it mean to you to remain in Christ like a branch in the vine (John 15:1–17)?

3. Is your life currently more like a flourishing tree or a dry bush in the wasteland? What's feeding your roots?
4. What pruning season have you gone through that later bore fruit?
5. When was the last time you stopped to intentionally marvel at a tree or any part of creation?

PRAYER OF THE DAY

God, thank You for the trees. Thank You for the beauty, breath, shelter, and lessons they offer. Help me remain in You like a branch in the vine. Nourish my soul with living water. Prune me when necessary. Root me in truth. And let my life bear fruit that brings You glory. May I never take for granted the miracle of Your creation or the sacrifice made on a tree for my salvation. In Jesus's name, amen.

WILDERNESS APPLICATION

- Sit beneath a tree and spend fifteen minutes in silence. Listen to the wind move through the leaves. Look up into its branches. Thank God for the gift of trees and reflect on the strength it takes to stand firm through seasons.
- Sketch a tree with its roots, trunk, branches, and fruit. Label each part with a symbol of your spiritual life (e.g., roots = trust, trunk = character, branches = calling, fruit = impact). What areas feel strong? What needs more attention?

- Read John 15:1–17 aloud while leaning against the trunk of a tree. Let the imagery sink in. Ask God to show you what it means to remain in Him today.
- Plant a tree—it could be a seed or a sapling—as a way of worshiping the Creator by stewarding His creation.
- Collect a fallen leaf, pine cone, or acorn. Place it somewhere you'll see it often. Let it remind you that you are rooted, you are growing, and you are connected to something far greater than yourself.

WILD TRASH

I'll never forget reading a survival story about a couple who became lost in the dense forests of Maine during winter. With nothing but the clothes on their backs, they walked for miles through frigid conditions, growing colder and more desperate by the hour.

Then, at the edge of an old logging road, they spotted a crushed disposable lighter, someone else's discarded trash.

Amazingly, the lighter could still produce a tiny spark. With some perseverance, they used it to ignite a bit of fluffy, dry grass. They nurtured that tiny flame into a fire, which saved them from hypothermia and kept them alive until rescue.

This story gives an entirely new meaning to the phrase "One man's trash is another man's treasure."

I hate seeing trash amid the raw beauty of nature. It seems I find it everywhere, even in places that feel impossibly remote. From glass bottles and deflated Mylar balloons to aluminum cans and broken gear, garbage finds its way into the farthest reaches of forests and deserts. But if I was a lost survivor at the end of my rope in any one of those places, you'd better believe someone else's trash would be a very welcome sight, regardless of how unsightly it might be.

A piece of reflective foil could signal for help. A rusted metal bucket could be used to boil water. A plastic bottle could carry it. After teaching survival skills for over twenty-five years and studying hundreds of real-life survival stories, I've learned firsthand that the mess left behind by one person could be the rescue tool for another.

This is also true in the wilderness of life.

Sometimes, the messes we walk through—including the pain, the mistakes, and the failures—feel like shameful garbage. We try to bury them or cast them alongside the pathways of life to be forgotten. We want to pretend these messes never happened.

Tragedy. Sickness. Bad decisions. Death. Infidelity. Accidents. Addictions. Debt. Divorce. Disaster. The list goes on forever.

But hiding our messes in life could very well rob someone else of the opportunity to pick up something that changes the course of their own journey through the wilderness. God has a way of redeeming even our worst moments. Just like with that broken lighter, God can use your broken past to spark hope in someone else.

Your struggle, your story, and your scars might be the very piece of "trash" that gives someone else the tools and the will to keep going. Your survival story can become their survival tool. If you're not dead, God isn't done!

There is nothing more powerful than hope. When you share your mess, it can become a message of hope to someone else. When you offer your past, God can turn it into someone else's pathway to healing. You may feel like your story tarnishes the beauty of what God is doing in the landscape of your life, similar to trash in the forest, but it might just be the light someone needs to find their way in the dark. As Romans 8:28 tells us, God can use it all: "And we know that in all things God works for the good of those who love him, who have been called according to his purpose." This includes the broken, messy, and painful parts of your life. That includes your "trash."

The apostle Peter is a powerful example of someone whose "mess" became a message. Peter denied Jesus three times at His most critical hour. This was a mistake that could have defined him in shame. But after the resurrection, Jesus redeemed Peter's failure and restored him. Peter went on to preach one of the most powerful sermons in history, leading thousands to faith on the day of Pentecost. His denial didn't disqualify him; instead, God used it to shape his humility, deepen his testimony, and fuel his mission.

The enemy wants you to stay ashamed. He wants you to stay silent. But God wants to help you turn your mess into your message, and sometimes that starts with a spark from the garbage heap of your past.

IN THE WILD

Verse to Contemplate

They triumphed over him by the blood of the Lamb and by the word of their testimony. (Rev. 12:11)

QUESTIONS FOR THE WILDERNESS JOURNAL

1. What part of your story feels like something better left buried?

2. Has God ever used a painful part of your past to encourage or guide someone else?
3. Is there "trash" in your testimony that you've been too afraid or ashamed to share?
4. What survival tools has God handed you through life's hardest seasons?

PRAYER OF THE DAY

Father, thank You for redeeming what the world sees as worthless. Show me how You can use my mess to carry Your message. Help me release shame, embrace healing, and offer my story for the good of others. Use my past, including every mistake, every scar, and every broken moment, to spark hope for someone else. In Jesus's mighty name, amen.

WILDERNESS APPLICATION

Go on a hike or walk through a natural area and bring a small bag with you. As you walk, collect any litter or trash you find. As you do, let each piece remind you of a part of your story you've tried to discard or hide. Pray over it. Then, when you return, throw the trash away but write down the story God brings to mind. Ask Him to show you how that broken part could help someone else survive their storm. One day, when He prompts you, share it.

WILD OBEDIENCE

I'll never forget reaching a point in my wilderness survival training business when I knew I had to go all in if I ever wanted to see it thrive. Up until that point, I was treating it like a very unprofitable hobby while working night shifts and odd jobs just to make ends meet.

Honestly, I don't know if I lacked faith in myself or faith in God. The truth is probably a lot of both. I was holding back. And because of that, I wasn't making the commitment necessary to take my business to the next level.

So, I started searching for land of my own, a permanent home for my training business. But I didn't have much money to work with. Then, one day, I stumbled upon a property that felt like something out of a dream.

It had once been a retreat facility built by General Motors for its factory executives. But the plant had since moved to Mexico, and the twenty-one acres, which included a forest, meadow, pond, creek, and swamp, had been foreclosed and abandoned for over a decade. A massive ten-thousand-square-foot lodge sat right in the center, waiting to be reborn into classrooms, bunk rooms, and dining space.

I had more sweat equity than cash, so I made an offer to the bank for just over $100,000, the most I could manage at the time. To my surprise, they accepted. With the help of my wife, my parents, my friends, and my community, we got to work. We transformed that abandoned retreat into Willow Haven Outdoor, my permanent wilderness survival training facility. Looking back, there's no doubt in my mind the Lord blessed me with that property. He opened the doors to make it happen, and I often joke that General Motors built that place for me without knowing it.

When we opened, my classes filled fast, with thirty students every weekend, some from all over the world. Going all in on that facility legitimized my business and forced me to either make it work or go under. I quit my part-time jobs and invested 100 percent of my time, energy, and heart into what I felt called to do. Going all in made all the difference.

But while I was going all in on my career, I wasn't going all in on my faith.

I believed in Jesus. I occasionally went to church. I prayed before meals. But if I'm being honest, I was the definition of a lukewarm Christian. Jesus was working in my life, but I wasn't giving Him all of me. My faith was the equivalent to my unprofitable survival hobby before I went all in.

But the Lord was far from done with me. In fact, he was just getting started, with a conviction and ask that shook me to the core. He was calling me to go all in, but this time, it was for Him. His call to my wife and me was clear and undeniable: Sell the property. Give it back. Donate the proceeds to the kingdom.

This wasn't just a building. It was everything I had built. And it was an idol I had put before the Lord. My identity was built upon this property and what it could do for me instead of upon the Lord. It was one of the scariest leaps of faith in my entire life, but we obeyed. We sold Willow Haven Outdoor and gave all the proceeds, nearly $700,000, to a ministry that invests in the lives, education, and character of children.

For the first time in my life, I went all in on my faith. And what happened next changed everything. Soon after, God gave me a new vision: WILD GOD survival courses.

They would blend survival skills with spiritual formation—solitude in creation, hands-on wilderness training, worship around the fire, and devotionals pointing people to Jesus.

It was the perfect fit, but there was just one problem. I had no property. Why would the Lord have me give away the very facility needed for the new vision He had just given me?

That was the question I was literally wrestling with in prayer one morning at a coffee shop.

"Lord, help me understand," I prayed. "Why would You do this?"

And then my phone rang.

It was my old neighbor, who owned hundreds of acres next to my old property, the one I had given to the Lord. He lived out of state and was calling out of the blue. After some small talk, he said this:

"My family's been praying about whether to sell the land. But we've decided we won't sell it if there is a way to use it to bring one more person to Jesus. And I felt like the Lord wanted me to call you. Do you have any ideas?"

I lost it.

This man was offering me access to hundreds of acres of pristine wilderness, everything I needed for WILD GOD events. The Lord didn't need me to own anything, He just needed my obedience.

That same week, I volunteered to teach a survival day at a Salvation Army teen camp on six hundred forested acres in central Indiana. After a full day of training, I gave an invitation to follow Jesus, and fifteen teens gave their lives to Christ.

The next morning, Major Marc Johnson, the divisional commander of The Salvation Army Indiana Division, drove me around the property in a golf cart. This property had it all, including bunkhouses, lakes, paved trails, and wilderness training areas.

He pulled up to a lookout point, stopped the cart, and asked, "Do you think you could use any of this for the kingdom?"

I drove home in tears.

But this story isn't just about me. It's about you. God wants to blow your mind with His goodness. He wants to wow you with His faithfulness. But first, He's asking to be first in your life.

We're reminded what God thinks about a lukewarm faith in Revelation 3:16: "So, because you are lukewarm—neither hot nor cold—I am about to spit you out of my mouth."

Jesus doesn't want your leftovers. He's calling you to go all in. He explains it clearly in Luke 9:23–24: "Whoever wants to be my disciple must deny themselves and take up their cross daily and follow me. For whoever wants to save their life will lose it, but whoever loses their life for me will save it."

Going all in is going to look different for you than it did for me. But it always starts with obedience and surrender. It can be hard to take those big steps of faith, but Proverbs 3:5–6 reminds us to "trust in the LORD with all your heart and lean not on your own understanding; in all your ways submit to him, and he will make your paths straight."

God may not give you the whole map, but He will direct your steps. And when you obey, He provides. In my experience, the bigger the leap of faith, the more powerful the showing of His grace and provision. Philippians 4:19 promises: "God will meet all your needs according to the riches of his glory in Christ Jesus."

The beauty of obedience is that it builds faith. When we are obedient and see God's hand at work, our faith grows. Then, we become more obedient. Soon, we're chasing obedience because there is nothing in this world like the rush of feeling the Lord move in our lives. Knowing you're being used for the kingdom is the greatest adrenaline rush of all time. Going all in is scary. But so is living your whole life lukewarm and wondering what could have happened if you had trusted God with everything. Don't miss out on the wild adventure of faith.

IN THE WILD

Verse to Contemplate

Whoever wants to be my disciple must deny themselves and take up their cross daily and follow me. (Luke 9:23)

QUESTIONS FOR THE WILDERNESS JOURNAL

1. Where have you been holding back in your walk with Jesus?

2. What's one area of your life He may be asking for full surrender?
3. Have you ever seen Him provide in unexpected ways after a step of obedience?
4. What would it look like for you to go all in?

PRAYER OF THE DAY

Lord Jesus, I don't want to live a lukewarm life. I want to go all in. Even when I don't see the path clearly, I want to trust You with every part of my life. Give me the courage to surrender, the faith to obey, and the strength to follow You wherever You lead. In Jesus's name, amen.

WILDERNESS APPLICATION

- Take a solo hike and bring a small stick to represent something God is asking you to surrender. Build a small fire and toss it in as a symbolic act of going all in.
- Go for a vision walk. Walk a trail and ask God, "What are You calling me to that I've been hesitant to obey?"
- Write down anything that comes to mind in your journal.
- Take a faith step. Identify one bold action step you can take this week toward full obedience, then take it.

WILD BREAD

In survival, there are four main priorities, called the Core Four. These are shelter, water, fire, and food. Food is a big category that encompasses many different skill sets, from trapping and fishing to active hunting and even long-term food storage. I love teaching these various survival food skills. One that I recently taught through my Survival Skill of the Month Club service is how to make hardtack.

Hardtack is a simple, long-lasting survival bread made with just flour, water, and salt. It has been called "soldier's bread," "sea biscuit," and "tooth dullers." For centuries, it sustained explorers, pioneers, sailors, and soldiers because of its durability and long shelf life. Sailors in the age of exploration lived on it during long voyages across the oceans. During the Civil War, Union and Confederate soldiers carried hardtack in their packs, often softening it in coffee or soup before eating. In fact, hardtack from the Civil War can still be found in some museums and is technically still edible.

Hardtack may not win any awards for flavor, but it kept people alive through meager times. Properly dried and stored, it can last for years, even decades. It is nearly indestructible when kept dry, and archaeologists have even found edible pieces over one hundred years old. It is calorie-dense and lightweight, making it ideal for rations. Because it is so hard, it often needs to be soaked in liquid before eating, and soldiers often joked about their teeth breaking on it.

If you'd like to make hardtack at home, it's very simple. Just follow this recipe:

Ingredients

2 cups flour (all-purpose works fine)

½ to 1 teaspoon salt

½ to ¾ cup water

Instructions

1. Preheat oven to the lowest temperature.
2. Mix flour, salt, and water until you form a stiff dough.
3. Roll the dough out into a slab about ¼ to ½ inch thick.
4. Cut into squares (about 3×3 inches).
5. Poke holes in each piece with a fork to help them bake evenly.
6. Place on a raised grate on a cookie pan and bake for thirty minutes.
7. Flip the pieces and bake another thirty minutes, until completely dry.
8. Cool and store in an airtight container.

Hardtack may be a good survival food for meager times, but according to Jesus in Matthew 4:4, no amount of hardtack will ever be enough: "It is written: 'Man shall not live on bread alone, but on every word that comes from the mouth of God.'" It's very clear that we are more than a physical body. There is also a spiritual side to us, and it is fueled by God's Word. Without it, Jesus says we cannot live. That's a very serious statement. Just as we would never starve ourselves of physical food (bread), we don't want to starve ourselves of spiritual food (God's Word) either.

When we don't eat, the consequences are real. They start off mild and then compound into dysfunctions that drastically affect our life. The same is true when we starve ourselves of spending time in God's Word. There are consequences. Below is a list of ways spiritual hunger has manifested itself in my own life. See if you recognize any of these signs in your own life right now.

Restlessness and emptiness. Even when life looks full on the outside, it's possible to feel unsatisfied on the inside. A popular phrase for this phenomenon is that nothing in the world can fill a "God-shaped hole" in our heart. Worldly food cannot satisfy spiritual cravings. Ecclesiastes 1:8 puts it this way: "All things are wearisome, more than one can say. The eye never has enough of seeing, nor the ear its fill of hearing."

Weakness in faith. Just as the body grows weak when it's starved of food, our spirit grows weak to stand firm against temptation when it is starved of God's truth. If we keep relapsing into sin and don't feel strong enough to resist the devil, this is a very strong sign that we are starving spiritually. Psalm 119:11 shows the solution: "I have hidden your word in my heart that I might not sin against you."

Loss of joy or peace. Anxieties creep in when God's Word isn't fueling hope in our life. God's truth is the ultimate source of hope, and the devil knows that we have nothing without hope. Philippians 4:6–7 tells us exactly what to do: "Do not be anxious about anything, but in every situation, by prayer and petition, with thanksgiving, present your requests to God. And the peace of God, which transcends all understanding, will guard your hearts and your minds in Christ Jesus."

Worldly cravings increase. When we aren't feeding our spirit by consuming God's Word, we often turn to entertainment, possessions, porn, or addictions in a desperate attempt to fill that spiritual void. For years, my addiction was work. I thought that if I worked more, wrote more books, and filmed more television shows, then I would be happy. The truth is that nothing from this world can satisfy something that the spirit longs for. Jeremiah 2:13 says it perfectly: "My people have committed two sins: They have forsaken me, the spring of living water, and have dug their own cisterns, broken cisterns that cannot hold water."

Lackluster prayer life. I used to always say things like "I'm a horrible prayer" and "Praying isn't my gift." What I learned through time in God's Word is that one's comfort level with prayer is directly proportionate to time spent reading Scripture. When words feel forced, when we forget to pray, or when we feel distant even while praying, it's likely because our soul is hungry for the right food.

Recognizing these hunger pains in your life can be humbling, but the good news is that relieving them is as easy as cracking open the pages of God's Word.

IN THE WILD

Verse to Contemplate

Jesus answered, "It is written: 'Man shall not live on bread alone, but on every word that comes from the mouth of God.'" (Matt. 4:4)

QUESTIONS FOR THE WILDERNESS JOURNAL

1. Which of the warning signs of spiritual hunger do you recognize in your life right now?
2. What worldly cravings do you tend to turn to instead of God's Word when you're spiritually empty?
3. How can you build a daily rhythm of feeding your spirit with Scripture, even if only for a few minutes at a time?

PRAYER OF THE DAY

Lord, thank You for being the bread of life and the source of true satisfaction. Forgive me for the times I've tried to fill my hunger with things that will never satisfy. Teach me to hunger and thirst for Your Word above all else. Strengthen my faith, renew my joy, and help me find peace in You alone. In Jesus's name, amen.

WILDERNESS APPLICATION

This week, try making a batch of hardtack. As you mix the flour, water, and salt, think about how simple ingredients can keep you alive for years if prepared the right way. Then, open your Bible and read a chapter from the book of John. Compare the difference: One bread can keep you alive for a season, but the other, the Word of God, will keep you alive forever.

WILD CAIRNS

Maybe it's my Scottish and Celtic heritage, but I've always enjoyed stacking rocks. Cairns, which are stacks or piles of stones, have been used since prehistoric times to mark trails, burial sites, and places of significance. The word *cairn* comes from the Gaelic term *càrn*, reflecting their widespread use in Scotland and other parts of the British Isles.

Before modern-day trail blazes, cairns were often used as trail markers. You still find them on trails all over the world. Whether using a stack of rocks or something else, trail markers are serious business when it comes to hiking. When I teach trailblazing in my survival courses, I emphasize that these markers can help you find your way back to a starting point and also assist rescue crews in locating you if you're on the move. A good survival trail marker should have three qualities:

1. It should look man-made to avoid being mistaken for something natural.
2. It should indicate the direction of travel.
3. It should have motion if possible. (A strip of emergency blanket can add motion to almost any trail marker.)

What I find incredibly interesting is that hardly anyone would consider doing a backcountry hike or even a several-hour road trip without reading a map, consulting a GPS, and carefully following the proper trail blazes or road signs set out ahead of time by someone who knows the route.

However, we often do the exact opposite with the journey we call life. It's not uncommon to wander through life without a clear destination, failing to look for or consider critical trail markers set before us along the way. I'm certainly guilty of this type of "life hiking." But we all know that no map, no path, and no trail markers is a recipe for getting lost real quick.

If you don't have a map, clear path, guide, or trail markers, the world will gladly fill those roles for you. Before you know it, you're reading someone else's map and are on a path you happened upon by coincidence. These consequences manifest themselves in a lack of purpose, a feeling of wandering through life, working what feels like a dead-end job, and experiencing little to no fulfillment and meaning. I've certainly been there.

The good news is that there is a map, a clear path, and trail markers to follow that lead to the life hike your soul desires—one that ends in peace, fulfillment, and clear purpose.

If you haven't already guessed it, the map is the Bible, the path is God's will, and the trail markers are the subtle (and sometimes not so subtle) affirmations of the Holy Spirit along the way.

It's true: God has not only mapped and prepared the perfect route for your life, but He has already blazed the trail for you every step of the way. Oftentimes, we're simply reading the map handed to us by the world and are just too busy to look for, let alone see and hear, God's trail markers that guide us along the right path.

I love what is written about God's plan for us in Psalm 139:13–16:

> For you created my inmost being;
>   you knit me together in my mother's womb.
> I praise you because I am fearfully and wonderfully made;
>   your works are wonderful,
>   I know that full well.
> My frame was not hidden from you
>   when I was made in the secret place,
>   when I was woven together in the depths of the earth.
> Your eyes saw my unformed body;
>   all the days ordained for me were written in your book
>   before one of them came to be.

God made us. God knows us. God knows what's best for us. His plan is far greater, more fulfilling, and more impactful than anything we could ever possibly dream up on our own. Jeremiah 29:11 reminds us, "'For I know the plans I have for you,' declares the Lord, 'plans to prosper you and not to harm you, plans to give you hope and a future.'" This sounds like the kind of hike I want to take. How about you?

I know all too well the nagging question, "What's God's plan for my life?" I've asked myself that question a million times. That is a big reason why I've written this devotional. But if you're asking yourself that question, you're missing the point, just like I was. The answer is much simpler than we believe it to be.

God's plan for you is for His will to be done in your life. This is the path to follow.

When asked how to pray, the first sentence of Jesus's reply in what is known as the Lord's Prayer is about God's will being done: "Our Father in heaven, hallowed be your name, your kingdom come, your will be done, on earth as it is in heaven" (Matt. 6:10).

But to follow a path, we need a map. This is where the Bible comes in. This is how we answer the follow-up question, "Okay, so if God's plan is for His will to be done in my life, then what is His will?"

The Bible is where God's will for us is revealed. Below are just a few verses that help clarify it:

> For my Father's will is that everyone who looks to the Son and believes in Him shall have eternal life, and I will raise them up at the last day. (John 6:40)

> For it is God's will that by doing good you should silence the ignorant talk of foolish people. (1 Pet. 2:15)

> "Love the Lord your God with all your heart and with all your soul and with all your mind." This is the first and greatest commandment. And the second is like it: "Love your neighbor as yourself." All the Law and the Prophets hang on these two commandments. (Matt. 22:37–40)

> Give thanks in all circumstances; for this is God's will for you in Christ Jesus. (1 Thess. 5:18)

But when it comes to God's will, this verse from Romans 12:2 is one of my favorites:

> Do not conform to the pattern of this world, but be transformed by the renewing of your mind. Then you will be able to test and approve what God's will is—his good, pleasing and perfect will.

These verses tell us that we will be able to discern God's will as we remain in and abide in Him. God's will becomes clearer as we grow spiritually. While there are many spiritual disciplines that can help with this growth process, three of the most important are

1. reading, studying, and contemplating God's living Word (the Bible);
2. praying (without ceasing); and
3. solitude (alone time between you and God, free from distractions).

The answer to the question "What is God's plan for my life?" hangs in the balance of seeking, praying, and striving for God's will in your life. This takes discipline, intention, commitment, fortitude, and next-level faith.

But while walking this path, just know that God has already blazed the trail before you. His spiritual cairns will not lead you to a wrong turn. Here are a few verses I have found to be encouraging on my own hike the past few years that are great ones to contemplate as you seek God's specific will for your life:

> The LORD himself goes before you and will be with you; he will never leave you nor forsake you. Do not be afraid; do not be discouraged. (Deut. 31:8)

> The steps of a man are established by the LORD, when he delights in his way; though he fall, he shall not be cast headlong, for the LORD upholds his hand. (Ps. 37:23–24 ESV)

> Your word is a lamp to my feet and a light to my path. (Ps. 119:105)

Just because God has planned and blazed the path for us doesn't mean there won't be pitfalls along the way. There will certainly be many to contend with. But we're never hiking alone, and He controls the path and everything on it.

So, to wrap this up, "What is God's plan for my life?" is the wrong question.

Instead, ask yourself:

- "How can I use my gifts, talents, finances, and influence to honor God today?"
- "How can I be more like Christ today?"
- "How can I love people today like Jesus did?"

If you've been struggling to discern God's will for your life, consider taking a few minutes to pray the same prayer that David did in Psalm 25:4–5:

> Show me your ways, LORD,
> teach me your paths.
> Guide me in your truth and teach me,
> for you are God my Savior,
> and my hope is in you all day long.

IN THE WILD

Verse to Contemplate

> Your word is a lamp to my feet
> and a light to my path. (Ps. 119:105 ESV)

QUESTIONS FOR THE WILDERNESS JOURNAL

1. Have you ever felt like you were "life hiking" without a map or directions? What were the results?
2. What are some spiritual cairns you've seen God place along your path recently?
3. Which of the three disciplines—reading Scripture, prayer, or solitude—do you most need to reintroduce into your life right now?
4. What's one practical way you can honor God with your gifts and influence today?
5. Are there any maps you've been following that weren't written by God?

PRAYER OF THE DAY

Lord, thank You for being a God who not only maps the trail but walks it with me. Help me to seek Your will above all else. Train my eyes to recognize Your trail markers and my ears to hear the Spirit's direction. Guide me in Your truth and teach me, for You are God my Savior, and my hope is in You all day long. In Jesus's name, amen.

WILDERNESS APPLICATION

- Go for a hike or walk and build a small cairn in a place that reminds you of God's faithfulness. Use it as a visual prayer.

- Draw or sketch your life path so far. Include moments of clarity, lostness, and when you felt God's direction most clearly.
- Choose one Scripture about God's will from this devotional and memorize it this week while spending time in creation.
- Practice fifteen minutes of solitude outdoors each day for the next three days. Use that time to listen and reflect on this question: "Where is God leading me next?"

WILD MULLEIN

Common mullein is one of the most remarkable plants God ever created. It's soft, sturdy, and packed with uses both practical and medicinal. The leaves are large, thick, and covered in fine, fuzzy hairs. While they feel soft to the touch, those tiny hairs can irritate the skin, so be careful. Despite their inviting fuzziness, resist the urge to use them as makeshift cowboy toilet paper, unless you're aiming for an itchy, irritated backside. For that particular use, moss is a much better choice. Interestingly, folklore tells us that in days gone by, women would rub the slightly irritating mullein leaves against their cheeks to create a natural blush.

Indigenous cultures recognized mullein's medicinal value long ago. Mullein was used to ease lung ailments like asthma and coughs. When smoked or brewed into tea, the leaves and yellow flowers help open airways and soothe inflammation. And when dried, those same leaves make excellent tinder. The tall, upright stalks are often dry and exposed to wind and are ideal for fire kindling. For this reason, the plant has even earned the nickname "the torch plant."

That name isn't metaphorical. At the tip of the mullein stalk, dried flower remnants form a bristled brush that can be several feet long. Indigenous people would coat this part in rendered animal fat, called tallow, which saturated the fibers and created a torch that could last upward of forty-five minutes. The mullein plant acted as a wick that burned the tallow as fuel. These torches lit the way for night fishing, camp tasks, and travel after dark. They didn't light the entire forest like modern headlamps do but provided just enough light for the next few steps. They were a dependable and readily available lighting option.

And that's exactly what God's Word is for us.

A mullein torch won't show you the whole path ahead. But it will guide your next step. So does Scripture. The Bible doesn't always give us the full blueprint for our lives, but it always illuminates the next faithful move. In a world full of noise, confusion, and pressure, God's Word is alive and active. And as 2 Timothy 3:16–17 describes, it guides us step-by-step, decision by decision: "All Scripture is God-breathed and is useful for teaching, rebuking, correcting and training in righteousness, so that the servant of God may be thoroughly equipped for every good work."

The Bible isn't just comforting, it's incredibly practical. It's our survival manual for life's wilderness. It shows us how to walk in truth, how to live wisely, how to make choices that honor God, and how to keep our footing when the terrain gets rough.

Looking back at my life, the biggest messes I've made have come from leaning on and trusting my own understanding. But Proverbs 3:5–6 reminds us to "trust in the Lord with all your heart and lean not on your own understanding; in all your ways submit to him, and he will make your paths straight."

You don't have to guess your way forward. You don't need to flip a coin. God has given you His Word to guide you, and His Spirit to speak through it. He is not hiding His will, He is waiting for you to open His Book so He can clearly reveal it to you. And alongside that revelation is refreshment, wisdom, joy, and enlightenment, as revealed in Psalm 19:7–8:

> The law of the Lord is perfect,
> refreshing the soul.
> The statutes of the Lord are trustworthy,
> making wise the simple.
> The precepts of the Lord are right,
> giving joy to the heart.
> The commands of the Lord are radiant,
> giving light to the eyes.

God's Word is both a torch and a map. And it's available to you right now. If you believe that God is wiser than you, and that His plans are better than yours, then your response is simple: Let His Word light your way.

A good life is made up of good steps, made one decision at a time.

And good steps come from God-lit paths.

IN THE WILD

Verse to Contemplate

> The precepts of the Lord are right,
> giving joy to the heart.

The commands of the LORD are radiant,
giving light to the eyes. (Ps. 19:8)

QUESTIONS FOR THE WILDERNESS JOURNAL

1. When was the last time you truly let Scripture guide a decision in your life? What was the result?
2. Are there areas in your life where you're currently walking without light, relying on your own understanding?
3. How do you typically respond when the full path ahead isn't clear? What might it look like to take just the next faithful step?
4. What habits or rhythms could help you stay more consistently in God's Word each week?
5. What verse or passage has been a guiding torch for you in past wilderness seasons?

PRAYER OF THE DAY

God, thank You for giving me Your Word. It is a steady, dependable light when the path ahead seems dark. Help me to trust You, even when I can't see far. Remind me that one step of obedience is better than a thousand steps of uncertainty on my own. Let Your truth anchor me, shape me, and lead me into Your will. Teach me to pause, listen, and follow. In Jesus's name, amen.

WILDERNESS APPLICATION

- After sunset, take a walk with only a flashlight or headlamp. Keep the beam focused at your feet, not far ahead. As you walk, reflect on how God's Word works the same way, providing just enough light for the next step.
- Write Psalm 119:105 on a small card or tag and clip it to your backpack, steering wheel, or mirror this week. Let it be a daily reminder to check in with Scripture before moving forward. Memorize it.
- Find or sketch a mullein leaf, which is shaped like the sole of a foot, and write one key verse inside the outline. Let this be your "step verse" for the week, guiding your next move.
- Challenge yourself to memorize a short passage of Scripture this week that you can mentally "strike" like a flint when you need direction. Start with Proverbs 3:5–6 or Psalm 19:7–8.
- Choose another short passage of Scripture and spend an entire week with it. Read it daily. Meditate on it during your hikes or commutes. Let it soak in slowly, lighting the path one step at a time.

WILD COMFORT

Several years ago, I was asked to take the stage to give a TED Talk. The title of my presentation was "How Survival Skills Bring About Personal Transformation."

The premise of this fifteen-minute talk was simple: When I take people into the wilderness for a survival experience, it's not very long until discomfort begins to set in. Exhaustion. Hunger. Thirst. Soreness. Minor injuries. Exposure to the elements. The annoyance of biting insects. The sheer overwhelm of having to provide for every human need from what the wild offers. Oftentimes, discomfort comes from a combination of many of these.

However, I've learned by taking hundreds of people into the wild that once they become uncomfortable and begin to struggle to meet their most basic survival needs (shelter, water, fire, food), something almost magical happens. That discomfort and struggle bring about a newfound perspective unlike anything else I've seen in the world. Suddenly, a simple drink of water becomes a blessing. One mouthful of food feels like a feast. One hour of solid rest is cherished. The sun's warmth on a cold winter day brings joy. The discovery of wild edible berries brings elation. The moment a spark catches on dry tinder fills the soul with pride. Even lying down on a bed of sticks and grass feels like a gift.

When you've clawed, scratched, and worked extremely hard for your most basic needs, your perspective changes. And with that new perspective comes deep appreciation, not just for the simple pleasures of home like a bed, a pot, a door, a window screen, or soap, but also for the people you love.

I've learned that the discomfort my students feel in the wilderness isn't from a lack of skill or poor instruction. It's simply that the wilderness is often uncomfortable. The interesting thing is, we are no more or less uncomfortable than our ancestors were. The only difference is, for them, discomfort was a constant companion.

We live in an era of unprecedented comfort. In the United States especially, we live better than the wealthiest kings in history, with abundant food and water, shelter, climate control, technology, instant entertainment, and instant gratification. The inconveniences we complain about today include slow Wi-Fi, late DoorDash deliveries, and cold coffee. These are a world apart from the survival threats our ancestors faced.

But the effects of our modern comfort run far deeper than unappreciation of conveniences. There are spiritual consequences of being comfortable that can undermine our dependence on and longing for God. Comfort can lull us into believing that this life is as good as it gets, dulling our hunger for the unimaginable things God has prepared for us: "No eye has seen, no ear has heard, no mind has conceived what God has prepared for those who love him" (1 Cor. 2:9).

Even the most breathtaking sunsets, the most comfortable beds, and the most extravagant vacations cannot compare to what God has waiting for His people. If we become too comfortable here, we lose sight of the fact that there is infinitely more ahead than we can imagine.

Just as in my survival courses, discomfort in life can become one of our greatest gifts. It's often in discomfort that we realize how dependent we are on the Lord and that we long for the day when He will wipe every tear from our eyes and erase every discomfort forever. Discomfort reminds us we're not made for this world. It awakens our inner longing for the "more" that God promises.

I've come to believe that creature comforts can be one of Satan's tools to lessen our dependency on the Lord. When we're not in pain, not struggling, and not doing without, we're tempted to rely on ourselves. We replace God's grace with more hustle, bigger paychecks, and new purchases.

Perhaps that's why Scripture speaks with such urgency about life's brevity: "Be very careful, then, how you live—not as unwise but as wise, making the most of every opportunity, because the days are evil" (Eph. 5:15–16). Comfort can lull us into spiritual sleep. This verse is a wake-up call, reminding us that time is short and the stakes are high. Every day is a chance to invest in eternal things before the opportunity slips away. Psalm 39 says it like this:

> Show me, Lord, my life's end
>   and the number of my days;
>   let me know how fleeting my life is.
> You have made my days a mere handbreadth;
>   the span of my years is as nothing before you.

Everyone is but a breath,
even those who seem secure. . . .
But now, Lord, what do I look for?
My hope is in you. (vv. 4–5, 7)

Even the most secure and comfortable life is a breath away from its end. David's prayer reminds us to shift our hope away from comfort and security in this life and to anchor it fully in God. James 4:14 rightfully compares our life to a mist: "What is your life? You are a mist that appears for a little while and then vanishes." Just like fog that burns away with the morning sun, our lives are temporary. Discomfort can strip away the illusion of permanence and remind us to focus on what will outlast this life.

When I take people out into the wilderness for a survival experience, whether it's two days or two weeks, my goal is never for them to be too comfortable. Because I know that life's greatest lessons for them—and the biggest takeaways, far beyond learning survival skills—will be how their perspective will be forever changed and how they will deeply appreciate and long for life back at home.

I can't help but believe that's a little bit like how our God thinks. Maybe His goal isn't for us to be too comfortable either. In the end, comfort might possibly be a tool of the enemy. The Bible's repeated warnings about the brevity of life and the numbering of our days may point to this very truth: Life is too short for us to be lulled into complacency by comfort.

IN THE WILD

Verses to Contemplate

Be very careful, then, how you live—not as unwise but as wise, making the most of every opportunity, because the days are evil. (Eph. 5:15–16)

QUESTIONS FOR THE WILDERNESS JOURNAL

1. How has discomfort in your life deepened your appreciation for God's provision?
2. What comforts in your life might be dulling your hunger for God?
3. How can you use seasons of struggle to grow closer to the Lord?
4. What would change in your life if you treated every day as a fleeting opportunity for eternal impact?

PRAYER OF THE DAY

Lord, thank You for the discomforts that remind me I am not made for this world. Forgive me when I cling too tightly to comfort and lose my hunger for You. Use every hardship to sharpen my perspective and turn my heart toward eternity. Help me walk wisely, making the most of every day You've given me. In Jesus's name, amen.

WILDERNESS APPLICATION

- Go without one comfort today, such as hot water, your phone, or a favorite snack. Let the absence sharpen your gratitude and draw your attention to God.
- Build a small fire with only what you can gather in the woods, and let its smoke remind you that life is short, like a mist that vanishes.
- Take a hike without music or podcasts. Let the silence become a space to talk with God about the comforts that may be dulling your dependence on Him.
- Sleep outside for a night, even in your backyard, without modern comforts. Reflect on how discomfort stirs a deeper longing for the eternal home God has promised.

WILD GOLIATH

I've always been infatuated with the story of David and Goliath. David, a young shepherd boy, went face-to-face with the giant Philistine soldier Goliath with a shepherd's sling and a few rocks. He defeated him with a well-placed stone to the head.

Shepherd slings were used by shepherds to protect the sheep from predators, like wolves. There is also a rich history of slings being used to hunt small game and even being used in battle. Sling bullets of all kinds, made from stone, clay, and even lead, have been found throughout the world.

I had the unique opportunity to learn how to weave a shepherd's sling from a well-respected primitive technologist. What I learned is that while this weapon is incredibly simple, it is very powerful. I got to see firsthand how it can be remarkably dangerous.

You've likely heard the story of David and Goliath before. It's one of the most well-known stories in the Bible, and I've heard it dozens of times throughout my life. My goal is to share some powerful insights that might make this story come alive in a new way for you.

David has seven older brothers. His three oldest brothers have followed King Saul to war against the Philistines, while David spends much of his time tending his father's sheep in Bethlehem. It quickly becomes clear that David's older brothers view his work as less important than theirs. After all, they hold a position that garnered honor and glory in those days: fighting on the front lines against the Philistines.

Yet, when David explains to Saul why he is prepared to face the giant Goliath, we see a remarkable declaration of faith and experience. In 1 Samuel 17:34–37, David says:

> Your servant has been keeping his father's sheep. When a lion or a bear came and carried off a sheep from the flock, I went after it, struck it, and rescued the sheep from its mouth. When it turned on me, I seized it by its hair, struck it, and killed it. Your servant has killed both the lion and the bear; this uncircumcised Philistine will be like one of them, because he has defied the armies of the living God. The Lord who rescued me from the paw of the lion and the paw of the bear will rescue me from the hand of this Philistine.

I don't know about you, but there have definitely been moments in my life when the work I was doing felt far from glamorous or even important. I can only imagine that David may have felt this way at times, shepherding sheep while his brothers were off doing what seemed to be more important work.

But don't miss this: God was preparing David for something special. By defending sheep from lions and bears, David was honing skills that would ultimately be used to bring immense glory to God. His season of preparation instilled in him the confidence needed for a defining moment in his life. We see in 1 Samuel 17:48–49, "As the Philistine moved closer to attack him, David ran quickly toward the battle line to meet him. Reaching into his bag and taking out a stone, he slung it and struck the Philistine on the forehead. The stone sank into his forehead, and he fell facedown on the ground." Notice that David ran toward the challenge God had put before him. He was ready for the moment God had called him to.

So, here's my encouragement for you today: It's easy to feel that what you're doing right now doesn't matter, that it's unimportant or without purpose. But God always has a plan.

God can use all the skills, knowledge, relationships, connections, and experiences you're gaining in this season to prepare you for something significant, just like David. Even tasks that feel mundane or insignificant can be used by God in extraordinary ways. As Ephesians 3:20–21 reminds us: "Now to him who is able to do immeasurably more than all we ask or imagine, according to his power that is at work within us, to him be glory in the church and in Christ Jesus throughout all generations, for ever and ever! Amen."

But there's something else to consider: David didn't wait to honor God until he faced Goliath. He honored God in the quiet, everyday moments of shepherding sheep.

For me, I've committed to honor God even in the mundane, and I look forward to running toward whatever challenge He calls me to in the future.

Your Goliath is just around the corner.

IN THE WILD

Verse to Contemplate

The LORD who rescued me from the paw of the lion and the paw of the bear will rescue me from the hand of this Philistine. (1 Sam. 17:37)

QUESTIONS FOR THE WILDERNESS JOURNAL

1. What shepherding work are you doing right now that feels overlooked but may be preparing you for something greater?
2. What are the lions and bears (past trials) God has already delivered you from? How do they build your faith for today's battle?
3. What is your current Goliath, and what five smooth stones (e.g., skills, truths, Scriptures, habits, mentors) has God already placed in your bag?
4. Where do you sense God inviting you to *run toward* the challenge instead of shrinking back?
5. How can you honor God in your quiet, ordinary tasks this week?

PRAYER OF THE DAY

Father, thank You for the unseen seasons of preparation. Teach me to honor You in the mundane and to recognize the skills You're shaping in me. Give me courage to run toward the battles You've called me to and faith to trust that the victory belongs to You. Use my past deliverances to fuel today's obedience. In Jesus's name, amen.

WILDERNESS APPLICATION

- Go to a creek or lakeshore and pick five smooth stones. On each, write one weapon God has given you (e.g., Scripture, prayer, courage, past testimony, community). Keep them somewhere visible this week.
- Practice a simple sling-style throw (safely, with a tennis ball, and aiming at a stump). Notice how precision comes from practice in small things, and journal about the parallel for your spiritual life.
- Do an ordinary task with holy intent (trail cleanup, gear maintenance, caring for animals). Pray as you work: *Lord, train my hands in the quiet for the battles I cannot yet see.*
- Read 1 Samuel 17 aloud and underline every verb tied to David's action (*kept, went, struck, rescued, ran*, etc.). Ask which action God is inviting you to take today.

WILD SOLITUDE

Several years ago, I hosted a television show called *Fat Guys in the Woods*. Each week I took three men into the wilderness for six days, often with just a knife and a canteen. We built shelters, made fires, found food, and lived off the land. The week was filled with laughter, tears, frustration, and small victories. We were often tired, hungry, dirty, sore, and homesick. And yet, many of those men still call it one of the best experiences of their lives.

One of the most powerful parts of the journey was the final night, when each participant struck out alone to spend a night in the woods. With only the skills they had learned, they built their own shelter and fire and endured the night in solitude. Almost every man told me later that this lonely night was the most impactful part of the experience. Many spent time thinking about their families, their goals, and their struggles. And several shared with me that they prayed for the first time in years.

Why is that? Because solitude in the wilderness has a way of stripping away distractions and opening our hearts to God. It is, after all, the place He originally designed to spend time with us in.

There is something sacred about the margin. Stepping away from schedules, noise, stress, and even family provides room to breathe, reflect, and listen. Solitude in the wild is not just about being alone; it also creates space for God's presence, encouraged by the creativity, majesty, and peace of God's creation.

At the height of His ministry, Jesus was surrounded by crowds everywhere He went. People followed Him for healing, teaching, and miracles. Yet even with the pressure of people's constant needs, Luke 5:16 tells us He made solitude a priority: "But Jesus often withdrew to lonely places and prayed."

The Gospels are filled with these moments. Before choosing His twelve disciples, Luke 6:12–13 tells us about another one of Jesus's solo trips: "One of those days Jesus went out to a mountainside to pray, and spent the night praying to God. When morning came, he called his disciples to him and chose twelve of them, whom he also designated apostles." Matthew 4:1–2 tells of Jesus heading into the wilderness for forty days before beginning His ministry: "Then Jesus was led by the Spirit into the wilderness to be tempted by the devil. After fasting forty days and forty nights, he was hungry."

Mark 6:31 says that later, after exhausting days of healing and teaching, "because so many people were coming and going that they did not even have a chance to eat, he said to them, 'Come with me by yourselves to a quiet place and get some rest.'" Another moment of solitude comes in Matthew 14:13, when Jesus learns of John the Baptist's death: "When Jesus heard what had happened, he withdrew by boat privately to a solitary place."

In John 6:15, Jesus also retreats to avoid distractions and stay focused: "Jesus, knowing that they intended to come and make him king by force, withdrew again to a mountain by himself." Jesus also sought solitude with the Father in the garden of Gethsemane on the night before His crucifixion. This is detailed in Matthew 26:39: "Going a little farther, he fell with his face to the ground and prayed, 'My Father, if it is possible, may this cup be taken from me. Yet not as I will, but as you will.'"

Why did Jesus withdraw so often? We learn through these various accounts that it was to pray and commune with God, to prepare for significant decisions, to rest and recharge, to grieve, to avoid distractions, to seek strength, and to align His will with God's. If the Son of God needed solitude to stay aligned with the Father, how much more do we?

Yet the world fights against this. Our days are filled with sports schedules, job demands, social media notifications, and endless entertainment. Even good things like church activities can crowd out time with God. It's almost as if the enemy knows solitude is powerful, transformative, and essential for walking closely with Jesus.

That's why I think of solitude in the wild not as being alone but as being alone with God. The point isn't emptying your mind, it's filling your soul with His Word, His Spirit, and His presence. Solitude in nature is where you can marvel at His creation, quiet your spirit, and hear His voice without interruption.

I like to think of it as a sacred rhythm, what I sometimes call *solutrinitas natura*: solitude with the Triune God in creation. It is time set apart to withdraw from the noise and reconnect with what truly matters.

I like to apply Paul's advice in 1 Thessalonians 5:16–18 to my wilderness solitude time: "Rejoice always, pray continually, give thanks in all circumstances; for this is God's will for you in Christ Jesus."

Wilderness solitude creates the margin to practice these commands in a unique way by rejoicing in creation, praying without distraction, and giving thanks with a full heart. You don't need six days in the woods with just a knife and a canteen to experience the benefits of solitary time with God. Even fifteen minutes outdoors can become a sacred appointment. I often use a simple framework: Marvel at creation, give thanks, and meditate on a short Scripture. This practice can slow you down, recenter your heart, and reconnect you with God in a way little else can.

I often say that if God repeats Himself in the Bible, it must be important. There's a reason we're told about Jesus's own solitude so many times. It is a critical spiritual survival skill.

IN THE WILD

Verse to Contemplate

> But Jesus often withdrew to lonely places and prayed. (Luke 5:16)

QUESTIONS FOR THE WILDERNESS JOURNAL

1. When was the last time you were truly alone with God in nature with no phone and no distractions?
2. Which distractions tend to crowd out your opportunity for solitude?

3. Do you struggle to believe that solitude is spiritually productive? Why or why not?
4. How can you carve out space this week for intentional wilderness time with God?
5. What would it look like to regularly practice *solutrinitas natura*?

PRAYER OF THE DAY

Father, thank You for the gift of solitude and the quiet places where You meet me. Teach me to withdraw not out of isolation but for intimacy with You. Help me to hear Your voice more clearly, to slow down, and to fix my eyes on what is eternal. Give me the discipline to create sacred margins in my life, and the courage to step away from the noise and into Your presence. In Jesus's name, amen.

WILDERNESS APPLICATION

Plan your own time of *solutrinitas natura* this week. Choose a nearby natural space—woods, a park, a trail, or even your backyard. Leave your phone behind. Take only a Bible, a journal, and a sense of expectancy. Use this framework:

- Marvel at creation: Find one wild thing to observe and reflect on God's creative power.
- Offer thanksgiving: Thank God for three things, including one that's currently hard.

- Meditate on Scripture: Choose a short passage and ask God to speak personally through it.

Let this sacred solitude reset your priorities and rekindle your connection to the Father. Like Jesus, find your quiet place—and return to it often.

WILD IMPOSTOR

When people see me on television, read one of my survival books, or hear me speaking confidently in interviews, they often assume I'm always sure of myself. But the truth is I've struggled with impostor syndrome for most of my life.

Impostor syndrome is the persistent belief that you're not good enough or qualified enough, and that at any moment someone will figure out you don't really belong where you are.

While it's gotten better over the years, I can still remember a time not that long ago when I felt like I was faking my way through everything in the survival world.

Who was I to be teaching survival skills?

I had never served in the military. I wasn't descended from a long line of rugged mountain men. I hadn't survived a year lost in the wild or lived through some harrowing expedition in the Amazon. When I taught my first class, all I had to show was a wilderness survival merit badge on my Boy Scout sash.

That's it.

I can vividly remember dreading questions from students, not because I didn't care but because I feared my answers were just my opinion. I didn't have a stack of credentials or degrees. Most of what I taught I had learned the hard way, through trial and error in the field.

Reading other survival books, watching more experienced instructors on TV, or scrolling through content online didn't inspire me, it made me feel less qualified. I feared saying the wrong thing or teaching a technique the wrong way. What if I didn't know the right answer? I had no mentor, no certification behind my name, no official stamp of approval. All I had was a deep passion for the outdoors and a calling I couldn't explain.

Even after decades of experience that included writing books, filming television shows, teaching thousands of students, and making appearances on national news outlets, the feeling never completely left. I've been teaching survival skills for over twenty-five years, and I still battle impostor syndrome.

And it doesn't stop with survival training. As I began surrendering more of my life to Jesus, that same feeling of inadequacy crept in again, but this time in my faith.

I had experienced a radical transformation in my life because of Jesus. I wanted to share it. I needed to share it with the people I taught, with those who followed my work, and with anyone who might listen.

But the doubts came flooding in:

Who are you to talk about faith?

You're not a preacher.

You're not a theologian.

You didn't go to seminary.

I'm just a wilderness survival instructor whose life was flipped upside down by the grace and love of Jesus. And the spiritual impostor syndrome hit hard. I questioned whether the Lord could really use me. I didn't feel worthy. I didn't feel ready. I didn't feel Christian enough to represent Jesus.

How about you?

Have you ever questioned whether God could use you?

Do you struggle with spiritual impostor syndrome?

Do you feel disqualified because of your past?

Do you feel too broken, too messy, too weak?

Do you feel like your faith is too small or your testimony too simple?

Does your lack of training or Bible knowledge make you feel unworthy to speak about Jesus?

Guess what?

You're reading a devotional written by someone who feels the exact same way. That means you're in great company. God loves using people like us. In fact, Scripture is full of people who felt just as inadequate. Here's just one example, from Jeremiah:

> "Alas, Sovereign LORD," I said, "I do not know how to speak; I am too young."
>
> But the LORD said to me, "Do not say, 'I am too young.' You must go to everyone I send you to and say whatever I command you." (1:6–7)

Jeremiah didn't feel qualified. He was young, inexperienced, and scared. But God reminded him that His calling trumps our credentials.

Remember Paul's thorn in the flesh in 2 Corinthians 12? Our weakness doesn't disqualify us. It actually makes room for God's strength to shine: "But [the Lord] said to me, 'My grace is sufficient for you, for my power is made perfect in weakness.' Therefore I will boast all the more gladly about my weaknesses, so that Christ's power may rest on me" (v. 9).

And then there was Peter and John. They weren't seminary grads. They were ordinary, unschooled men. But their courage came from being with Jesus and from the power of the Holy Spirit. That's what matters. "When they saw the courage of Peter and John and realized that they were unschooled, ordinary men, they were astonished and took note that these men had been with Jesus" (Acts 4:13).

First Corinthians 1:27–29 reminds us that God chooses weak things to glorify His strength. He intentionally uses the underqualified to show that it's Him working, not us: "But God chose the foolish things of the world to shame the wise; God chose the weak things of the world to shame the strong. . . . So that no one may boast before him" (vv. 27, 29).

Even Moses told God he wasn't a good speaker.

Even Noah thought he was too old to build a boat.

And we know how those stories turned out.

When you feel underqualified to stand up for your faith, just remember that obedience trumps credentials all day long. As Jesus tells His disciples, "When they arrest you, do not worry about what to say or how to say it. At that time you will be given what to say, for it will not be you speaking, but the Spirit of your Father speaking through you" (Matt. 10:19–20).

When it comes to your witness, your job isn't to be eloquent—it's to be obedient. Take the first step. God will meet you there.

As Ephesians 3:20 illustrates, we can lean on him for the heavy lifting; God "is able to do immeasurably more than all we ask or imagine," but we have to be willing to be used.

You're not an impostor. You're a masterpiece in progress. And as Ephesians 2:10 promises, God has good works prepared specifically for you: "For we are God's handiwork, created in Christ Jesus to do good works, which God prepared in advance for us to do." Whatever your story, whatever your training, whatever your failures, whatever your background, God can use it all for His glory.

Spiritual impostor syndrome isn't just doubting yourself. It's doubting God. So suck it up, take the first step, and let Him do the rest. That's all He needs to do something wild.

IN THE WILD

Verse to Contemplate

> Don't let anyone look down on you because you are young, but set an example for the believers in speech, in conduct, in love, in faith and in purity. (1 Tim. 4:12)

QUESTIONS FOR THE WILDERNESS JOURNAL

1. Where do you feel most like an impostor in your spiritual life right now?

2. What would it look like to give that insecurity to God today?
3. Can you think of a time when God used your weakness for His glory?
4. What's one step of obedience God may be asking you to take, even if you don't feel qualified?
5. Who in your life needs to hear your story, just the way it is?

PRAYER OF THE DAY

Lord Jesus, I often feel like I'm not enough—like I don't know enough, do enough, or believe enough. But I know You are enough. Help me to trust that You can use my life, not because I'm perfect, but because You are powerful. Let my weakness be a canvas for Your strength. I surrender the feeling of being an impostor, and I step forward in obedience, trusting You to speak and move through me. In Your name, amen.

WILDERNESS APPLICATION

- Go for a solo hike. At each mile, speak aloud one part of your testimony. Practice telling it raw and real.
- Etch *Ephesians* 2:10 or 1 *Timothy* 4:12 into a walking stick or stone. Let it remind you that you were made for and are prepared for this.

- Share something you've learned the hard way with someone younger in the faith or in life. Don't wait to be ready. You already are.
- Pray for boldness and ask God to give you one opportunity this week to share your faith, even in a small, casual way. Then go for it.

WILD MONARCH

Remember that childlike imagination you had as a kid, when you saw magic in simple things? I'd like to summon that back for a moment.

Monarch caterpillars begin their lives as tiny eggs on the milkweed plant, where they spend their entire first life consuming only the bitter parts of the plant. For about two weeks, they gorge themselves on milkweed, growing from the size of a grain of rice into striking black, white, and yellow–striped caterpillars. Then, something extraordinary happens—something that no amount of science can ever fully explain, recreate, duplicate, or even comprehend.

The caterpillar spins a small patch of silk, attaches itself upside down to a branch or structure, and hangs in a J-shape for about a day. Inside, something unbelievable is happening. After a period of preparation, the outer skin splits away as the caterpillar writhes and twists. Beneath it lies a brilliant green chrysalis, now enclosing the caterpillar like a burial cloth. But it gets even more astonishing.

As the chrysalis hardens over the next several hours, a delicate golden band appears around its surface like a thin, shining crown. It is breathtaking, so intricate and beautiful that it left me speechless when I once saw it happen right before my eyes. Over the next ten days, the caterpillar inside undergoes a radical transformation.

It liquefies, turning into an unrecognizable cellular soup. This is no mere change; it is a complete breakdown and reformation into something new. The complexity and intricacy of what happens within that chrysalis defy explanation. It is one of the most extraordinary wonders of creation, and calling it special is an understatement.

Somehow, within that liquid form, a monarch butterfly takes shape. Toward the end of the transformation, the chrysalis turns transparent, giving the rest of creation a glimpse of the miracle inside. Finally, the moment arrives when the chrysalis opens, and a vibrant-winged monarch emerges. As it stretches its wings to dry, you realize something remarkable: This butterfly is a completely new creation.

There is nothing about it that resembles its old self.

- It has changed colors.
- It has developed intricately scaled wings.
- It has grown a different number of legs.
- It has gained a completely new body structure.
- It has even transformed its diet, no longer consuming bitter milkweed but drinking the sweet nectar of flowers.

In every way, it is a new creature.

And unlike its first life, spent clinging to a single bitter plant, it now launches into a vast world, soaring toward the lush gardens of Mexico, where millions of other newly transformed monarchs—miracles of nature just like it—gather.

It's almost hard to believe something like this happens right here on earth, and it's just a bug!

What if God, the Creator of the heavens and the earth, designed parts of His creation to tell us a story and reveal a deeper truth about the spiritual journey of our souls? What if the monarch butterfly is a living parable of our own transformation in Christ?

Before we go further, consider these verses from Psalm 19:

> The heavens declare the glory of God;
> the skies proclaim the work of his hands.
> Day after day they pour forth speech;
> night after night they reveal knowledge.
> They have no speech, they use no words;
> no sound is heard from them.
> Yet their voice goes out into all the earth,
> their words to the ends of the world. (vv. 1–4)

Creation itself testifies about the glory of God. Could it be that God is speaking to us through the monarch's transformation? What if the milkweed plant symbolizes Earth, a tiny speck in the vastness of the universe? What if the bitter taste of milkweed represents the struggles, hardships, and trials of this life? What if the sweet nectar the butterfly now enjoys represents the abundance and joy of the life to come?

What if this echoes our own transformation in Christ?

> Therefore, if anyone is in Christ, the new creation has come: The old has gone, the new is here! (2 Cor. 5:17)

What if the caterpillar liquefying inside of the chrysalis is a reflection of what Jesus meant when He called us to lay down our lives and take up our cross daily?

> Whoever wants to be my disciple must deny themselves and take up their cross daily and follow me. For whoever wants to save their life will lose it, but whoever loses their life for me will save it. (Luke 9:23–25)

What if that golden ring around the chrysalis foreshadows the crown of glory awaiting those who remain faithful to Christ?

> And when the Chief Shepherd appears, you will receive the crown of glory that will never fade away. (1 Pet. 5:4)

Just as the monarch caterpillar cannot comprehend the journey that awaits it, what if we, too, cannot fathom the magnitude of what God has prepared for those who love Him?

> What no eye has seen, what no ear has heard, and what no human mind has conceived—the things God has prepared for those who love him. (1 Cor. 2:9)

What if following Christ truly changes us from the inside out, just as the caterpillar is transformed beyond recognition?

> And we all, who with unveiled faces contemplate the Lord's glory, are being transformed into his image with ever-increasing glory, which comes from the Lord, who is the Spirit. (2 Cor. 3:18)

What if, despite the moments of happiness and fulfillment we experience on earth, the best is yet to come? What if God's plan for our lives mirrors the monarch's migration and is more beautiful and vast than we could ever imagine?

> For we are God's handiwork, created in Christ Jesus to do good works, which God prepared in advance for us to do. (Eph. 2:10)

What if the difference between the caterpillar's bitter milkweed diet and the butterfly's sweet nectar diet is a picture of how God's Word nourishes us spiritually?

> Man shall not live by bread alone, but by every word that comes from the mouth of God. (Matt. 4:4)

What if true transformation requires a firm anchoring in God's truth, just as the caterpillar must anchor itself securely before the transformation begins?

> The Lord is my rock, my fortress and my deliverer; my God is my rock, in whom I take refuge, my shield and the horn of my salvation, my stronghold. (Ps. 18:2)

What if transformation is painful and uncomfortable? The caterpillar struggles as it sheds its old skin and liquefies inside the chrysalis. Change is never easy. But it's always worth it.

> Therefore we do not lose heart. Though outwardly we are wasting away, yet inwardly we are being renewed day by day. For our light and momentary troubles are achieving for us an eternal glory that far outweighs them all. (2 Cor. 4:16–17)

What if the monarch butterfly's journey is just one of countless revelations woven into creation, each a reminder of our eternal life with Jesus? What if we've been surrounded by messages from God all along, hidden in the things we pass by without a second thought?

IN THE WILD

Verse to Contemplate

Therefore, if anyone is in Christ, the new creation has come: The old has gone, the new is here! (2 Cor. 5:17)

QUESTIONS FOR THE WILDERNESS JOURNAL

1. In what area of your life do you sense God calling you into transformation?
2. Are there milkweed seasons in your story that have been bitter, uncomfortable, or preparatory? What did they teach you?
3. What would it look like to surrender fully to God's process, even if it means discomfort or breaking down old patterns?
4. How have you seen God's beauty and truth reflected in creation? What stood out?
5. What might it mean for you to take flight in this next season of your faith?

PRAYER OF THE DAY

Creator God, thank You for the story You've written into the wings of the monarch. Thank You that You don't just improve us, You completely remake us. Help me to anchor my life to You, to trust Your process even when I don't understand it, and to emerge from every season more like Jesus. Transform me from the inside out. May I one day soar with joy, beauty, and purpose into the future You've prepared. In Jesus's name, amen.

WILDERNESS APPLICATION

- Go for a walk in a field or garden and look for a butterfly, especially a monarch. Watch it closely. Let its flight remind you that your story is still unfolding and that God is doing something beautiful in your life, even if it's unseen.
- Draw or sketch the stages of the monarch's transformation, including egg, caterpillar, chrysalis, and butterfly. Label what each stage represents in your spiritual journey.
- Find a small object in nature to represent your chrysalis season. Carry it with you this week as a reminder that God is working in you, even when you feel still or hidden.
- Visit a patch of milkweed and reflect on a difficult season you've come through. What beauty or growth came from it?
- Spend ten quiet minutes outside and ask God this simple question: "What are You trying to transform in me right now?" Then wait, listen, and write down what comes.

WILD SMALLS

When I was starting my wilderness survival business, I did a lot of odd jobs to make ends meet. One of the most memorable was selling T-shirts at outdoor events and festivals. It wasn't glamorous, but it gave me the flexibility I needed to teach survival skills without being chained to an employer's schedule.

During that time, I met some truly unique characters, many of them fellow vendors who made their living working these circuits. One in particular left a lasting impression on me. He ran a booth called Junkitiques. It was a packed little corner of randomness, filled with odds and ends priced anywhere from one to three dollars.

I'll never forget how he explained his business strategy to me.

"Creek," he said, "I never sell twenty-dollar or fifty-dollar items. I make my living with the smalls, one dollar at a time."

That stuck with me. Not just in business but in survival and eventually in my walk with Christ.

I've used that same phrase, "the smalls," many times in my survival trapping and hunting courses. The truth is, in a survival situation, you'll rarely have the opportunity to take down a big animal like a wild boar or elk. Those chances are slim, and the skills, energy, and tools required make them an unlikely goal in a real survival context, especially without significant experience.

You're much better off going after the "smalls," such as frogs, fish, birds, rabbits, and crayfish. These are more abundant, easier to catch, and far more likely to provide the nourishment you need to survive. A string of small wins is the real strategy when you're living off the land, especially short-term.

And the same is true in our spiritual life.

When I first surrendered my life to Christ, there was no massive overnight transformation. I wasn't suddenly a Bible scholar. I couldn't quote Scripture on demand. I struggled to pray without feeling awkward. I didn't wake up every day overwhelmed with a sense of God's presence. And honestly, I had a hard time hearing His voice.

What did change was my perspective, and slowly, over time, my habits began to follow.

And maybe that's where you are right now. Maybe you've committed your life to Christ, but you still feel like you're stumbling through your prayers, unsure of your spiritual footing. Maybe you're waiting for a big moment to arrive, some dramatic spiritual milestone, but all you're experiencing is a string of small, seemingly unimpressive steps.

Don't overlook the power of "the smalls."

Spiritual maturity doesn't usually come in a lightning strike or a burning bush. It comes through small, consistent disciplines repeated daily, hourly, and sometimes minute by minute over a long stretch of time. The transformation you're longing for is found in the ordinary, faithful moments: reading the Word in the quiet of morning, offering short but sincere prayers, choosing gratitude when it's hard, noticing God's fingerprints in creation, and being generous when no one sees.

These are the spiritual smalls that add up to big changes. Galatians 6:9 encourages us to stay consistent, because our small, faithful efforts are not wasted. In time, they will yield something beautiful: "Let us not become weary in doing good, for at the proper time we will reap a harvest if we do not give up."

Hebrews 12:11 encourages us in the moments when it feels like nothing is changing and we have to dig deep with perseverance: "No discipline seems pleasant at the time, but painful. Later on, however, it produces a harvest of righteousness and peace for those who have been trained by it."

The truth is discipline doesn't feel transformational in the moment. It feels small. But, as Proverbs 21:5 puts it, the slow and steady work of diligence, spiritually or physically, is the strategy that pays off: "The plans of the diligent lead to profit as surely as haste leads to poverty."

Psalm 100 offers a great suggestion for two powerful spiritual smalls that can dramatically change your life over time: "Enter his gates with thanksgiving and his courts with praise; give thanks to him and praise his name" (v. 4). Praise and giving thanks are simple acts of worship that align your heart with God's will.

Just like I tell my survival students, it's exciting to think about bagging a big elk. But in reality, consistently gathering the smalls over time is the surest strategy for sustaining yourself in the wild. In the same way, it's not only the mountaintop spiritual moments that nourish us. Building a rhythm of small, daily acts of worship becomes a steady source of strength, drawing us into God's presence and slowly aligning our will with His.

IN THE WILD

Verse to Contemplate

Let us not become weary in doing good, for at the proper time we will reap a harvest if we do not give up.
(Gal. 6:9)

QUESTIONS FOR THE WILDERNESS JOURNAL

1. Are you expecting a spiritual big moment while overlooking the power of daily disciplines?
2. What small spiritual habits could you commit to this week?
3. How have you seen God use small, ordinary moments to bring transformation in your life?
4. Are you growing weary in doing good? What encouragement can you draw from Galatians 6:9?
5. What would your faith look like if you focused on spiritual smalls each day for a year?

PRAYER OF THE DAY

Heavenly Father, thank You for reminding me that spiritual growth doesn't require big, dramatic moments. You work through small acts of obedience, discipline, and trust. Help me not to grow weary in doing good, even when I don't see immediate results. Give me the patience to keep going, the perseverance to keep trusting, and the faith to believe You are growing something inside of me through the smalls. Teach me to walk with You every day, one step at a time. In Jesus's name, amen.

WILDERNESS APPLICATION

- Choose one spiritual small (e.g., morning prayer, a gratitude list, or reading a psalm) and do it daily for seven days. Reflect on the impact.
- Set up a figure 4 deadfall trap outdoors. The figure 4 deadfall is a survival trap that uses three sticks in the shape of a number four as a trigger that holds up a heavy weight, such as a rock. As you build it, think about how God builds transformation in you, piece by small piece.
- Go outside and find the smallest living thing you can, such as a bug or leaf. Thank God for using small things to teach big lessons.
- Take a short walk and list ten small things you're grateful for. Speak each one aloud as an act of worship.
- Each day, write one small spiritual victory (e.g., prayed instead of worried) on a slip of paper and place it in a jar. Watch how quickly it fills up.

WILD WILLOWS

I love my basket willows. I ordered the starts from a farm in Canada and planted about a dozen different varieties in a marshy area by my pond. I've meticulously curated those willow trees to produce dozens of thirty-six-inch flexible young willow shoots each season that can be harvested and used in courses for weaving baskets of all varieties.

The first year, the short one-inch stumps (about the diameter of a #2 pencil) that I stuck into the soft earth only produced a couple of spindly shoots. In the fall, I pruned the young willows down to within one inch of the ground. Miraculously, the next spring, they produced several more much healthier new shoots. After several years of doing this, each of those tiny little stumps produce dozens of perfect five-to-six-foot willow shoots that can be used for weaving baskets. They're awesome and the envy of any survival instructor.

The irony is that I have to aggressively prune a healthy basket willow almost down to the ground if I want it to produce more and better weaving shoots that can serve me well during the next teaching season. I'm sure the willows don't appreciate this at the time, but I have a very special purpose for their existence. They will impact hundreds of people and be made into amazing baskets that will last a very long time!

Without my purposeful pruning, they will quickly become messy, overgrown, and unhealthy. To be fruitful basket willows and produce a harvest, they need the continual discipline of my pruning. Without it, they're a mess.

We are like my basket willows. Without God's thoughtful pruning, we'll never bear the fruit He intends. As painful as it might be, we need to be pruned.

Looking back, I can see God's careful pruning in my life. One example, I believe, is my first television show, *Fat Guys in the Woods*. While the show was incredibly successful, the priorities in my personal life were upside down. To put it in basket willow terms, my willow shoots were disjointed, crooked, and weak.

When that television show was canceled, my pride was deeply hurt. But, looking back, it was the best possible thing that could have happened to me, my family, and my relationship with Christ. Soon thereafter, I began the difficult but freeing process of surrendering parts of my life to Christ. My career had become an idol. Success had become my god.

No matter how you look at it, pruning is painful. Whether God does it or you have the steel to do it yourself, it is short-term discomfort for long-term benefit. Pruning involves removing things in our lives that hinder our spiritual growth. These can include unhealthy relationships, behaviors, or other distractions. In John 15:1–8, Jesus shares some important insight about pruning:

> I am the true vine, and my Father is the gardener. He cuts off every branch in me that bears no fruit, while every branch that

> does bear fruit he prunes so that it will be even more fruitful. You are already clean because of the word I have spoken to you. Remain in me, as I also remain in you. No branch can bear fruit by itself; it must remain in the vine. Neither can you bear fruit unless you remain in me.
>
> I am the vine; you are the branches. If you remain in me and I in you, you will bear much fruit; apart from me you can do nothing. If you do not remain in me, you are like a branch that is thrown away and withers; such branches are picked up, thrown into the fire and burned. If you remain in me and my words remain in you, ask whatever you wish, and it will be done for you. This is to my Father's glory, that you bear much fruit, showing yourselves to be my disciples.

Notice that God is in charge of keeping the garden. He has the tools, experience, and know-how to manage the garden and every plant in it. He planted the garden and now tends it. Jesus is the true vine and the only vine that matters.

Galatians 5:22–23 tells us exactly what the fruit of the Spirit looks like: "The fruit of the Spirit is love, joy, peace, forbearance, kindness, goodness, faithfulness, gentleness and self-control. Against such things there is no law." If the fruit in our lives doesn't look like this, then we will be cut off from the vine (Jesus), which is the source of everything good. But even if our life does bear fruit, God will still prune it to help bear more fruit. Being pruned is a good thing. It means we must already be bearing some kind of fruit because God only prunes branches that are already producing fruit.

The key to bearing fruit is remaining in Him. This means to live a life attached to the living vine who is Jesus. Alone, we cannot bear fruit. The fruit God bears through us isn't about us; it is to bring glory to Him.

God has an awesome plan and purpose for our lives! He prunes those things that prevent us from stepping into that perfect plan. It is sometimes very hard to see the positive side of pruning while it is happening, like when my television show was suddenly canceled, but Hebrews 12:5–6 offers some comfort to consider: "My son, do not regard lightly the discipline of the Lord, nor be weary when reproved by him. For the Lord disciplines the one he loves, and chastises every son whom he receives" (ESV).

If you're being pruned, God loves and believes in you.

IN THE WILD

Verses to Contemplate

> I am the true vine, and my Father is the gardener. He cuts off every branch in me that bears no fruit, while every branch that does bear fruit he prunes so that it will be even more fruitful. (John 15:1–2)

QUESTIONS FOR THE WILDERNESS JOURNAL

1. Can you identify a time in your life when you were pruned by God? What fruit eventually grew from that painful season?
2. Is there anything in your life right now, such as relationships, habits, or distractions, that God may be trying to prune?

3. How do you normally respond to God's discipline or redirection?
4. What does remaining in the vine look like in your current season?
5. What kind of fruit would you like to see God grow in your life over the next year?

PRAYER OF THE DAY

Lord, I confess that pruning hurts. But I know You are the Gardener, and You only cut away what hinders my growth. Help me to trust Your hands even when the shears feel sharp. Remove anything in me that does not bear fruit. Root out idols, distractions, and misplaced priorities. I want to remain in You and bear much fruit, not for my glory, but for Yours. Thank You for loving me enough to refine me. In Jesus's name, amen.

WILDERNESS APPLICATION

- Gather a bundle of flexible living branches, willow if available, and try weaving them into a simple circle or coil. As you bend each shoot, reflect on the ways God has shaped and redirected you in life. Ask Him to keep you usable, flexible, and surrendered to His design.
- Walk through a wooded area or field and look for signs of healthy versus overgrown plants. Notice what has been

cut back, what's thriving, and what's wild and tangled. Reflect on how pruning makes growth more fruitful, even when it feels like a setback.

- Use pruning as a spiritual practice this week. Clean out your schedule, your workspace, or even your phone notifications. Ask God to show you what branches in your life need trimming so your energy can go toward what truly matters.

WILD FIBERS

While filming the show *SOS: How to Survive* for The Weather Channel, I studied a story of a couple who had become lost on a very rocky mountain during what was supposed to be a simple hiking trip. In their decision to move down the mountain to try to find their way back, they cascaded several steep cliffs, some as tall as fifteen feet.

On one occasion, they climbed down a cliff only to realize they couldn't continue forward. But when they tried to go back, they found they couldn't climb up the cliff they had just come down. They were trapped in a small, rocky area with very limited resources.

My job as the survival instructor host was to offer ideas they could have used to improve their situation and teach survival skills using what they had. In this particular case, they did have a backpacking tent. I started by cutting the tent into long, thin strips. Once fully deconstructed, that tent provided hundreds of feet of material. Individually, each strip was incredibly weak. It couldn't hold more than a pound or two before tearing. But

I used an ancient survival skill called the reverse wrap to turn these strips of nylon fabric into a climbing rope.

Indigenous cultures have used this process for generations, twisting and reverse twisting plant fibers, tree bark, and even grasses to form strong ropes. In fact, the Inca Empire used this very method to reverse wrap eighteen-inch mountain grasses together to form massive bridges. These bridges spanned hundreds of feet across deep canyons and were strong enough for people and animals to walk across.

The reverse wrap process is all about turning weakness into strength. By twisting individual fibers together, their combined force becomes exponentially stronger than any one strand on its own.

After reverse wrapping those nylon tent strips, I created a rope strong enough to hold my entire body weight. I cut a forked stick from a nearby pine tree growing on the cliff's edge and attached it to one end as a makeshift grappling hook. I threw it up the fifteen-foot cliff and around a sturdy branch. That rope, made from weak fibers, held me as I climbed out.

Let that sink in: A bunch of weak fibers, together, became strong enough to lift me to safety.

In Ecclesiastes 4:9–12, we're reminded of something very similar:

> Two are better than one,
>   because they have a good return for their labor:
> If either of them falls down,
>   one can help the other up.
> But pity anyone who falls
>   and has no one to help them up.

Also, if two lie down together, they will keep warm.
    But how can one keep warm alone?
Though one may be overpowered,
    two can defend themselves.
A cord of three strands is not quickly broken.

This is an incredible visual of what it means to be part of the body of Christ. As believers, we are just like those individual fibers. On our own, we can be fragile and weak. But together, twisted and wrapped in relationship, community, and truth, we're much stronger. The lesson of the reverse wrap isn't just about wilderness survival. It's about our life in Christ. We were never designed to do this alone.

I'll never forget when my marriage was in the dumpster, right on the brink of failure. The tactics of the enemy were crystal clear: keep me isolated from the people who loved me. And it worked. Shame and guilt kept me from community with other believers. I pulled away from those I knew would speak truth into my life.

We are especially vulnerable in isolation, just like those weak fibers. First Peter 5:8 warns us of what is waiting for us: "Be alert and of sober mind. Your enemy the devil prowls around like a roaring lion looking for someone to devour." If you've ever watched *National Geographic* footage of lions hunting, you know their tactic is to divide and conquer. They don't attack the herd. They strategize to get one animal separated and alone. That's when they strike.

Satan works the same way. He loves to isolate us. Because when we're isolated, we're vulnerable. When we're surrounded by the body of Christ, we're strong. Shame is an emotion the enemy uses as a strategy to keep us isolated.

But as Hebrews 3:13 outlines, there is strength in encouragement by other believers: "Encourage one another daily, as long as it is called 'Today,' so that none of you may be hardened by sin's deceitfulness."

Encouragement and accountability are the spiritual version of the reverse wrap. You're wrapping yourself with the strength of others and of Christ. The believers around you help guard your heart from drifting. They speak truth and lift you up when you can't lift yourself. Or, like Proverbs 27:17 puts it, "As iron sharpens iron, so one person sharpens another."

You grow stronger, wiser, and more faithful in community, not apart from it. The lone wolf strategy is not biblical and will most certainly end in failure.

Whether you're walking down a trail or navigating the wilderness of life, make an intentional effort to reverse wrap your life with others who love Jesus. It's not a sign of weakness. It's wisdom. And as Scripture clearly shows, it's how we stand strong against the schemes of the prowling enemy.

IN THE WILD

Verse to Contemplate

Though one may be overpowered,
two can defend themselves.
A cord of three strands is not quickly broken.
(Eccl. 4:12)

QUESTIONS FOR THE WILDERNESS JOURNAL

1. Are you walking through life with others, or are you going it alone?
2. Have you isolated yourself, maybe even subtly, due to shame or discouragement?
3. Who are the spiritual fibers around you who you can lean on, and who can you strengthen today?

PRAYER OF THE DAY

God, thank You for the strength of community. Thank You that You've designed me not to do this life alone. Help me resist the pull of isolation. Show me who I need to reach out to and who I can encourage today. Wrap me in truth and surround me with people who love You. In Jesus's name, amen.

WILDERNESS APPLICATION

- Learn the reverse wrap with natural fibers or cordage. As you twist each one, thank God for the people He's placed in your life.
- Text or call one believer who sharpens your walk with Christ. Thank them. Pray with them. Strengthen the rope.
- At your next group, pass out short cord strips and have everyone reverse wrap them together as a

symbolic activity, then read Ecclesiastes 4:9–12 aloud. A great material to use for this is raffia palm fibers, which are available in the craft section at most retailers.

WILD ENCOUNTER

A few years ago, I was a guest on *The Doctors* talk show to provide expert commentary for a story about a young woman who had a wild encounter with a grizzly bear. In fact, she was attacked while on a day hike. After knocking her to the ground, leaving her bloody and battered, the bear finally walked away. When she attempted to get up, it came back and attacked again, nearly killing her. I was asked what someone should do to survive an encounter with a grizzly bear. The protocol is straightforward.

If you encounter a grizzly, remain calm, avoid direct eye contact, and back away slowly. Your goal is to remove yourself as a threat. Grizzlies, unlike black bears, respond to aggression with aggression. If attacked, lie face down on the ground to protect your vital organs and lock your hands behind your neck to protect your neck. Keep your backpack on if you have one to protect your back. Try not to let the grizzly flip you over. Once the grizzly bear thinks the threat is neutralized, then it should leave. Don't get up until the bear is out of sight, or it might come back again.

While I've never been face-to-face with a grizzly, I, too, recently had one of the wildest encounters of my life. But it wasn't with an animal. In fact, the place and circumstances were quite ordinary. I was sitting at home on the couch with my wife on a random Tuesday evening.

To give you context, I must first tell you a story of what happened several months before this random Tuesday.

I was writing my latest disaster preparedness book (*Disaster Survival 101*) at the coffee shop at my church when my cell phone rang. I picked it up, and the man on the other end identified himself as an officer with the Hamilton County Sheriff's Department. He gave me my mailing address and asked if I lived there. I explained that I had recently moved to a new address, but yes, that was my old address.

He then told me I had two warrants out for my arrest due to failing to appear in court for two federal jury summonses. I told him I probably didn't receive them because I had moved. He said that didn't matter, and I needed to explain that to the judge in court. He said I needed to come to their office to pay the fine and also spend seventy-two hours in jail.

I'm not going to lie, I was freaking out inside. I started thinking about how I'd explain this to my wife, kids, and aging parents.

When I asked for the station address, the officer explained that due to the Covid pandemic, they now had an online payment option. He asked if I'd like to use that instead. I said no and insisted I'd like to pay the fine in person. As he gave me the street address, my cell phone lost connection.

Shaken up, I called my wife and told her I needed to go to jail, asking if she would come pick me up. I could hear my son, River, crying in the background. I, too, was on the verge of tears.

While I waited for my wife to arrive, I called the sheriff's office back to get the complete address and explained why I needed it.

The lady on the phone apologized and told me I had been scammed.

I felt foolish and angry. I was mad that my wife and kids had also been hurt. I was reminded that the world is full of broken people who do things like this.

Over the next several weeks, I recovered, of course, but I never forgot it.

Fast-forward to the random Tuesday evening when my wife and I were sitting on the couch. My phone rang. I picked it up, and the man on the other end identified himself as an officer with the Hamilton County Sheriff's Department.

Although it was a different voice than the last time, I immediately knew it was the same scam. My blood began to boil as my body and mind prepared to fight. As he outlined the same offense as the last call, I started forming my own response, filled with some choice words and ridicule I'd rehearsed in my head many times. I put my phone on speaker so my wife could hear me go to verbal war.

But just as I was about to unleash my fury, something extraordinary happened. Honestly, it's very difficult for me to describe. I felt the Holy Spirit calm me and the Lord whisper, "I want you to ask to pray with him."

Noticing the sudden change in my demeanor, my wife asked if I was okay.

I wasn't. The Lord asked me to do something that was very much out of my comfort zone and the complete opposite of what I wanted to do. My heart began pounding out of my chest, and I started to sweat.

The Lord had been working in my life, but, deep inside, I knew this was a defining moment in my faith. Would I obey or ignore?

I took a deep breath, interrupted the "officer" on the other end, and said, "Listen, man, this is going to sound a little weird, but please don't hang up. Would you mind if I prayed with you?"

You could hear a pin drop, and my wife's eyes were as wide as baseballs. I was sweating through my shirt.

After a few seconds, the man replied, "Yes."

You know how some people are great at praying? Their prayers sound fluid and confident, like they know exactly what to say? Well, that's not me. I'm actually a really horrible and awkward prayer. But I closed my eyes, asked the Holy Spirit for guidance, and said something like this:

"Lord, I don't know this man, but I know that You love him enough to send Your Son to die for him, and You have a plan and purpose for his life far greater than he could ever imagine. If he'll let You, You can use his gifts and talents to change eternity. Father, whatever the circumstances are that have caused him to feel he needs to make these calls, I ask that You move in his life in a powerful and undeniable way to help him get out of it and start living a life that aligns with Your will and honors You. In Jesus's name I pray, amen."

For a second, I thought he hung up. Then, something miraculous happened. I heard him start to cry.

I said, "Listen, man. I'm not mad at you, and I forgive you. It's not random that you called me tonight. God loves you, and I love you. He has incredible plans for your life, plans that you can't even fathom."

He openly cried and replied, "You don't know my situation."

I said, "I don't, but God does, and He is the God of the impossible. In fact, He loves the impossible."

I felt as if lightning was surging through my veins. The presence of the Holy Spirit was so palpable it was overwhelming.

I continued, "I'm not going to lie to you. It's not going to be easy, but it'll be worth it. God designed you on purpose and for a purpose, and this isn't it."

"I know it's not," he replied between sobs.

I said, "I'll commit to praying for you every day for the rest of my life. I'll pray that you'll step into God's plan for your life and that He binds any influence that threatens to keep you from doing so."

By this time, we were both crying. It was a big mush fest. I told him I loved him. He told me he loved me. I ended the call with this:

"I can't wait until the day I learn of all the amazing things God does in and through you. Your story is just beginning, and God can use your mess to be a powerful message, just as He's done with me. Clearly, you have my phone number. Call me if you ever want to pray together or need a pep talk."

Moments like these remind me of the powerful words in Philippians 2:13: "For it is God who works in you to will and to act in order to fulfill his good purpose."

Without that first scam call, which caused so much emotional stress to me and my family, I would never have had the context needed for my second call with him. God works in the craziest ways, and there is no better feeling than knowing you're a part of it.

I can't help but wonder how many wild encounters like this I've missed in my life because I've been so focused on the seen rather than the unseen.

What wild encounter does God have up His sleeve for you today? Trust me, you do not want to miss it.

IN THE WILD

Verse to Contemplate

For it is God who works in you to will and to act in order to fulfill his good purpose. (Phil. 2:13)

QUESTIONS FOR THE WILDERNESS JOURNAL

1. Have you ever had an encounter that seemed random at first, but later you realized God was in it?
2. What distractions or frustrations in your life might actually be divine appointments in disguise?
3. When was the last time you clearly felt the Holy Spirit prompt you to do something uncomfortable? How did you respond?
4. Are there people in your life whom God might be asking you to forgive or pray with, just like I did with the scam caller?
5. What would it look like for you to be spiritually prepared for a wild encounter this week?

PRAYER OF THE DAY

Father, I don't want to miss a single encounter You've planned for me. Help me slow down, listen, and obey, especially when it's uncomfortable. Thank You for showing up in unexpected places and for using even the messiest moments for Your glory. Teach me to walk by faith, not by sight, and give me the courage to respond when You whisper, "This is your moment." I want to live with open eyes, a soft heart, and hands ready to serve. In Jesus's name, amen.

WILDERNESS APPLICATION

- Go for a walk or hike with no headphones or distractions. Ask God to give you a divine appointment, even if it's just a moment of clarity.
- Write down a list of interruptions from your week. Which ones might have been wild encounters in disguise?
- Pick up a small stone and write a name on it, someone God may be calling you to pray for or reach out to. Carry it in your pocket as a reminder.
- Practice active obedience. Choose one uncomfortable act of obedience, like reaching out to someone difficult, forgiving someone, or sharing your faith. Do it today.
- Journal a prayer asking God to use you in someone else's redemption story, just as He used me in the scam caller's story.

WILD CATCH

My grandfather in Kentucky taught me one of the best fishing tips of all time when I was just about ten years old. Carrying simple cane poles and bare hooks, we had walked down the hill from his house to the branch that ran through a rocky bed in the valley nearby. The slate-bottomed creek was beautiful and teeming with life. It had many perfect swimming holes, and it was a rock hound's dream. The entire branch and creek bottom were covered in all the sorts of rocks you could possibly imagine. Long ago, there was a Native American village nearby, and if you were lucky, you would find an arrowhead with its own story to tell.

But the best part about this branch was the bluegill fishing. There were pockets of bluegill in that creek like I've never experienced since. It was a little boy's dream. But when we arrived, I had one pressing question:

"Grandpa, what are we using for bait?" We hadn't brought any.

Without missing a beat, he reached into his pocket, pulled out his pocketknife, and showed me a plant growing along the creek bank—giant ragweed. It had massive palmate leaves and thick, rigid stalks. He explained we were looking for the stalks with swollen, knobby growths, caused by a parasitic insect laying its eggs inside. Over time, larvae would hatch, burrow into the stalk, and create these telltale bulges.

One by one, we carefully carved open the stalks to find fat white larvae, which served as juicy little baits that were absolutely irresistible to those Kentucky bluegill. That day, we caught so many fish we roasted a few right there on the rocky shoreline and still brought home plenty more for a family fish fry the next day. That bait changed everything.

In Luke 5:1–11, Peter, James, and John had a very different kind of fishing experience:

> One day as Jesus was standing by the Lake of Gennesaret, the people were crowding around him and listening to the word of God. He saw at the water's edge two boats, left there by the fishermen, who were washing their nets.
>
> He got into one of the boats, the one belonging to Simon, and asked him to put out a little from shore. Then he sat down and taught the people from the boat.
>
> When he had finished speaking, he said to Simon, "Put out into deep water, and let down the nets for a catch."
>
> Simon answered, "Master, we've worked hard all night and haven't caught anything. But because you say so, I will let down the nets."
>
> When they had done so, they caught such a large number of fish that their nets began to break. So they signaled their partners in the other boat to come and help them, and they came and filled both boats so full that they began to sink.
>
> When Simon Peter saw this, he fell at Jesus' knees and said, "Go away from me, Lord; I am a sinful man!"

> For he and all his companions were astonished at the catch of fish they had taken, and so were James and John, the sons of Zebedee, Simon's partners.
>
> Then Jesus said to Simon, "Don't be afraid; from now on you will fish for people." So they pulled their boats up on shore, left everything and followed him.

In the story with my grandpa, having the right bait—and knowing how to find it—made all the difference. But for Peter, James, and John, the thing that made all the difference was when Jesus entered the scene. When Jesus showed up, everything changed.

The bait didn't matter.

The conditions didn't matter.

The environment didn't matter.

Their skills didn't matter.

The only two things that mattered were

1. Jesus's presence, and
2. the obedience of the fishermen.

Jesus took a long, unproductive day of fishing and turned it into one of the most unforgettable catches of their lives. That moment wasn't just about the fish. It was about revealing who Jesus is and what can happen when we listen to Him, even when it doesn't make sense and it goes against everything we think we know.

This was just the beginning of all the amazing things they would witness Jesus do. And even more amazing, what He would later do through them.

This story reminds me of John 14:15: "If you love me, keep my commands."

Throughout Scripture, obedience is a theme tied directly to love and trust. So often, it's easy to forget that one of the most basic and foundational aspects of following Jesus is simply doing what He asks.

In Luke 5, Jesus didn't demand a theology degree or a perfect past. He simply gave clear instructions—"Let down the nets"—and Peter responded with "Because you say so" (vv. 4–5). That one act of trust and obedience changed everything.

Obedience isn't about religious performance or trying to earn favor, it's about surrendering to the leadership and sovereignty of Jesus, even when we can't see the outcome. We can try all night in our own strength and still come up empty. But when He speaks, and when we obey, the miraculous becomes possible.

In our lives, Jesus still speaks. He speaks through Scripture. He speaks through the Holy Spirit. He speaks through prayer. And often, he speaks through the simple nudges we feel when we're quiet and listening. We're not as lucky to have Him come right to our workplace and speak to us like He did to Peter, John, and James, but He still speaks. And He's laid out His commands for us clearly in Scripture.

These commands are, of course, timeless and written in black and white: "Love the Lord your God with all your heart and with all your soul and with all your mind and with all your strength" and "Love your neighbor as yourself" (Mark 12:30–31).

Other times, they're specific to our life, our calling, and our moment.

Speak up.

Forgive.

Give.

Stay.

Go.

James 1:22 has very specific advice about God's commands: "Do not merely listen to the word, and so deceive yourselves. Do what it says."

We can get caught up in the distractions and noise of this world, but obedience is often quiet, consistent, and unseen. Clear examples of obedience include spending time in the Word, practicing solitude, praying daily, loving when it's hard, giving when it costs us, and obeying when it doesn't make sense. It's in those moments that we set the stage for miracles, not because we earned them but because we simply made room for God to work.

IN THE WILD

Verse to Contemplate

Master, we've worked hard all night and haven't caught anything. But because you say so, I will let down the nets. (Luke 5:5)

QUESTIONS FOR THE WILDERNESS JOURNAL

1. Where in your life have you fished all night and come up empty?
2. What is Jesus asking you to do today that doesn't make sense at first glance?

3. Is there a small step of obedience you've been delaying? Why?
4. What spiritual discipline do you need to pick back up to sharpen your hearing for God's voice?
5. When was the last time you saw a miraculous catch as a result of simply obeying?

PRAYER OF THE DAY

Dear Lord, I confess that I often rely on my own skills, timing, and understanding. But You call me to trust You. Speak, Lord, and help me respond with a willing heart. Help me obey quickly, even when I don't understand the outcome. I know You can do more with one act of obedience than I could do with a lifetime of striving. I want to be ready when You say, "Let down your nets." In Jesus's mighty name, amen.

WILDERNESS APPLICATION

- Go fishing using the simplest setup you have. Let it remind you that skill and bait don't matter as much as obedience and trust.
- Write down one act of obedience God is prompting you to take. Do it today.
- Spend fifteen minutes in outdoor solitude listening for the gentle direction of the Holy Spirit.

- Draw a picture of a net overflowing with fish. Around it, write the names of people or areas in your life you're trusting Jesus with.
- Read Luke 5:1–11 slowly each morning this week in your outdoor solitude. Each day, ask, "What are You saying to me, Lord?"

WILD FOCUS

While filming an episode of *SOS: How to Survive*, I covered the story of a couple who had gotten lost in the wilderness while on what was supposed to be a short day hike. One wrong turn led to another, and before long, they found themselves cold, lost, and without shelter, fire, food, or water. But they did have a few everyday items on them, one of which was a camera.

As the host of the show, my job was to demonstrate ways they could have used the items they had on hand to increase their chances of survival. In this case, I showed how they could use a rock to smash open the digital camera, retrieve the small glass lens, and use it to focus the sun's rays to create fire.

I'll never forget filming that demonstration. The camera lens was small, maybe a half inch in diameter, and made from curved glass. To get a fire going, everything had to be perfect. The sun had to be out and high in the sky. The tinder had to be dry. In this case, I used a piece of dry rabbit poop I'd found on location. (Note: Dry rabbit poop is an amazing solar fire tinder.) But most importantly, I had to hold the lens in absolute, unwavering alignment with the sun. Any shake, any slight tilt, and the light would scatter. I had to remain perfectly still under the blazing midday sun for several minutes until that tiny point of focused light finally caused the rabbit pellet to smoke and a smoldering ember to form. A few minutes later, I had a tinder bundle in full flame. This was the beginning of a fire that, in a real survival scenario, could save your life.

Without focus, none of it would've been possible.

And that's not just true for survival fire starting in the wilderness, it's also true for our walk with Jesus.

Just like Hebrews 12:1–2 reminds us: "Let us run with perseverance the race marked out for us, fixing our eyes on Jesus, the pioneer and perfecter of faith."

It is critical to keep our eyes locked on the end goal. But the world is full of distractions. Endless responsibilities, digital noise, worries, and temptations are all constantly trying to pull our attention in every direction but the one that matters most. But just like that lens, when we align our hearts and minds directly toward the Son, something powerful begins to happen. Our focus becomes fuel. Our stillness becomes strength. And what was once dry and lifeless in us can begin to smolder into fire. This is a fire for God, His Word, His kingdom, and His people.

Focus alone isn't enough. The object of our focus matters. Colossians 3:2 says it very clearly: "Set your minds on things above, not on earthly things."

But the world wants us to focus on careers, personal goals, financial security, politics, and culture. However, Matthew 6:33

promises: "But seek first his kingdom and his righteousness, and all these things will be given to you as well."

Without that eternal focus, we drift. The light scatters. We lose heat. We lose direction. But when we lock in on Jesus, everything else begins to fall into place.

We are the lens. All we have to do is face the Son.

IN THE WILD

Verses to Contemplate

> Let us run with perseverance the race marked out for us, fixing our eyes on Jesus, the pioneer and perfecter of faith. (Heb. 12:1–2)

QUESTIONS FOR THE WILDERNESS JOURNAL

1. What's currently pulling your focus away from Jesus?
2. Can you remember a time when your faith felt sharp and clear? What brought that focus?
3. What distractions, such as habits, thoughts, or routines, need to be set aside to regain clarity?
4. What areas of your life are dry tinder waiting to catch fire with the right spiritual focus?
5. How can you reframe your daily rhythms to intentionally align with the Son?

PRAYER OF THE DAY

Lord, the world is noisy and full of things that pull my attention in every direction. But I want to fix my eyes on You. Help me focus. Still my heart. Align my thoughts and actions with Yours. Like a lens fixed on the sun, may my life catch fire as I center it on the Son. Let that fire burn bright and pure—not for my sake but for Your glory. In Jesus's name, amen.

WILDERNESS APPLICATION

- Go outside with a magnifying glass and try to start a small fire with the sun. If conditions allow, observe how important stillness and alignment are to success.
- Sit in nature for ten minutes with no distractions. Practice stillness. Let the wind, birds, and sunlight quiet your mind as you refocus on Jesus.
- Find a sunlit spot and read aloud each of the verses from this devotional. Let them soak in as truth and guidance.
- As you go about your day, whisper this phrase as a prayer: "Fix my eyes, Lord." Let it recenter you every time you feel distracted.

WILD STRENGTH

On some level, we all connect strength with survival. Maybe it's that old phrase "survival of the fittest" we learned in school. But real strength doesn't always look like what we expect.

I recently returned from an incredible WILD GOD survival course. These three-day courses are packed with hands-on wilderness training, such as building shelters, making fires, and learning to live with the land. But just as importantly, we set aside time to honor the Creator who made all of it possible. It was a rhythm of skill, solitude, worship, and, of course, plenty of fire.

At this recent course, I met a couple who reshaped my understanding of strength. Each morning of the course, Randy and Michele slowly made their way from the bunkhouses to the wilderness camp about a quarter mile away. Randy matched his pace to Michele's, steady and protective, while Michele refused every offer of a ride in our Kawasaki Mule. Back in 2018, doctors told her she'd never walk again after being diagnosed with multiple sclerosis.

As I watched them approach, I honestly wondered whether she'd be able to tackle some of the more demanding skills on the schedule, like bow drill fire starting, which is a challenge that tests even the fittest of participants. But God had a lesson waiting for all of us.

Step after step, task after task, Michele kept moving forward. Again and again, we heard her say, "It's all God. It's God's grace. My strength is the Lord's. Thank you, Jesus. Praise God." Her words weren't clichés; they were her lifeline. Beside her, Randy stood strong like a sturdy oak, steady and watchful, his eyes filled with pride as he supported his wife.

Michele embodied the truth of Psalm 84:5: "Blessed are those whose strength is in you, whose hearts are set on pilgrimage."

Someone on a pilgrimage isn't focused on the short term. They're in it for the long haul and know that the journey only exists because of the destination. Michele reminded us of this as she placed one foot in front of the other, every step a declaration that her strength came not from her body, but from the Lord.

A pilgrim's path is never easy. Trails must be blazed, elements battled, and difficult terrain overcome. Each of us has a pilgrimage to make in this lifetime. The question becomes, Whose strength are we relying on?

Even bow drill fire making teaches us that it isn't brute force that produces the ember, but a steady rhythm, patience, and endurance. The same is true in faith. Human willpower alone cannot carry us through the hard places. But when our strength is rooted in His Spirit, everything changes. The road may not be easier, but it becomes marked with blessings in the midst of trials. Like Michele, every step became a blessing in her life because her strength was in the Lord.

Michele's story was a living picture of this truth. Although told she'd never walk again, she pressed forward, leaning into God for every ounce of strength. And like the oak-strong presence of Randy beside her, God often places people in our lives to steady us when we falter. Just as Paul describes in 2 Corinthians 12:9, our testimony can reveal that strength isn't the absence of weakness, it's God showing up in the midst of it: "But he said to me, 'My grace is sufficient for you, for my power is made perfect in weakness.' Therefore I will boast all the more gladly about my weaknesses, so that Christ's power may rest on me."

A heart set on pilgrimage knows this life is just the proving ground for the next. Jesus of course set the ultimate example in enduring the journey to the cross for our sins. First Corinthians 9:24 reminds us to keep our eyes on the prize ahead: "Do you not know that in a race all the runners run, but only one gets the prize? Run in such a way as to get the prize."

Set your heart on pilgrimage and lean on His strength to see you through every obstacle along the way.

IN THE WILD

Verse to Contemplate

Blessed are those whose strength is in you,
whose hearts are set on pilgrimage. (Ps. 84:5)

QUESTIONS FOR THE WILDERNESS JOURNAL

1. Where are you tempted to depend on your own strength instead of God's?
2. What pilgrimage are you walking right now that feels uphill and exhausting?
3. Who has God placed beside you, like Randy for Michele, to steady you in your walk?
4. How might your weakness today become the very place where God's strength shines brightest?

PRAYER OF THE DAY

Lord, I confess that I often try to rely on my own strength. But I know real strength comes only from You. Help me see weakness not as failure but as the doorway for Your power. Thank You for the companions You've placed in my journey. Give me endurance for the climb, courage for the valleys, and joy for the pilgrimage. In Jesus's name, amen.

WILDERNESS APPLICATION

- Take a slow, intentional hike, noticing how your steps require both strength and balance. Use it as a reminder of God's strength in your weakness.
- Attempt a survival skill that challenges you, like bow drill fire making or shelter building, then reflect

on how persistence and reliance mirror spiritual endurance.

- Rest under a tall oak tree and consider the oaks in your life, the people who have steadied you when you felt weak. Thank God for them.
- On your next outdoor trek, leave a marker stone at a bend in the trail as a reminder that your strength is not in you, but in the Lord.

WILD CHASE

I'll never forget my first real survival adventure. It was very early in my survival training. I had decided to test my skills in the wild for real.

It was a cold October weekend, and I headed out into the woods with nothing but a knife on my hip. The sun was shining, but I knew it was going to get cold. I had only worn a heavy wool sweater and wool pants, and so not only did I need shelter, but I needed a sufficient fire. But I was a survival instructor, so my pack overflowed with plenty of ego.

I spent most of the afternoon building my lean-to shelter. That was where I made my first mistake—not building my fire first. Shelter building was exhausting. My undergarments were wet with sweat. The sun was beginning to drop along with the temperature. My confidence was deflating as well.

I tried every fire start I knew. I carved a bow drill set but wasn't successful. I carved a hand drill set, but it didn't give me the ember I needed. I tried to strike my knife against a piece of flint I found in the bed of a creek, but the tiny sparks wouldn't smolder the natural tinder I had gathered. I tried everything

I could think of, and nothing gave me the fire I so desperately needed. Nothing was working like in my controlled backyard environment.

Whether I second-guessed myself or whether it was a nudge from the Lord, I had put a disposable lighter in my pocket earlier that day. And after all other things had failed and the sun had entirely set, I humbly used the lighter to ignite the dry tinder and get a fire going.

When all of my own ideas had failed, I fell back on the one sure thing I knew would work. If I had it to do all over again, I would have just used the lighter in the beginning. To this day, I always say in my survival classes that I teach bow drill fire starting and flint-and-steel fire starting so that people understand you never really want to put yourself in a position where you have to depend on those things for fire.

The irony of this story is that my faith walk mirrors this scenario almost exactly. Maybe you can relate.

I tried all the things in life to fulfill me. I chased success in my career and business. I chased fame on television. I chased notoriety in writing over forty wilderness survival and disaster preparedness books. I chased authority in appearing on dozens of national news channels and morning shows. Yet none of them offered the fulfillment or lasting happiness I was searching for.

It was only when I chose the one true source of fulfillment that I began to have peace in my life. This guaranteed source of fire was, of course, a fully surrendered life to Jesus.

The Bible has a lot to say about chasing the things of this world, and it's filled with people who have walked that same path before us. Ecclesiastes 2:10–11 is a great start: "I denied myself nothing my eyes desired; I refused my heart no pleasure. My heart took delight in all my labor, and this was the reward for all my toil. Yet when I surveyed all that my hands had done and what I had toiled to achieve, everything was meaningless, a chasing after the wind; nothing was gained under the sun." Even the wisest and wealthiest man of his time, King Solomon, discovered that worldly pursuits, without God at the center, are empty and fleeting.

Jeremiah 2:13 tells another story of people going it on their own: "My people have committed two sins: They have forsaken me, the spring of living water, and have dug their own cisterns, broken cisterns that cannot hold water."

When we turn to the wells of this world for satisfaction, they eventually run dry. Only God offers a source that never fails. And for those of us who insist on digging our own wells, Jesus has this to say: "Everyone who drinks this water will be thirsty again, but whoever drinks the water I give them will never thirst. Indeed, the water I give them will become in them a spring of water welling up to eternal life" (John 4:13–14).

The world's pleasures always fade. Jesus gives a living water that satisfies our deepest thirst for all eternity. First John 2:15–17 says it another way: "Do not love the world or anything in the world. If anyone loves the world, love for the Father is not in them. For everything in the world—the lust of the flesh, the lust of the eyes, and the pride of life—comes not from the Father but from the world. The world and its desires pass away, but whoever does the will of God lives forever."

The desires of this world pass away, but a life anchored in Christ lasts forever.

I was so good at the chase that I lost sight of what really matters. The irony of all of this is that the chase never satisfies. True happiness, peace, and satisfaction come from allowing yourself to be caught, to surrender, and to allow your heart to be captured by the One who knows it best.

IN THE WILD

Verse to Contemplate

> Whoever drinks the water I give them will never thirst. Indeed, the water I give them will become in them a spring of water welling up to eternal life. (John 4:14)

QUESTIONS FOR THE WILDERNESS JOURNAL

1. What fires in your life have you been trying to start with your own strength instead of going to God first?
2. What worldly pursuits have you chased that ultimately left you empty?
3. How do you know when you're relying on your own methods instead of trusting the Lord?
4. What would it look like to go straight to the lighter in your faith walk, to go directly to Jesus in every need?
5. In what areas of your life do you still need to fully surrender to God?

PRAYER OF THE DAY

Lord, I don't want to waste my life chasing after things that can't satisfy. I confess that I've often gone to the world's solutions before coming to You. Teach me to seek You first, to trust You fully, and to drink deeply from the living water only You can give. Capture my heart completely, Lord, and let my satisfaction be found in You alone. In Jesus's mighty name, amen.

WILDERNESS APPLICATION

- Start a fire with your most reliable method first, whether that's a lighter, matches, or ferro rod. As the flames grow, reflect on the difference between going straight to a sure source of warmth versus wasting energy on what *might* work.
- Go for a walk near a water source—a river, creek, or spring. Watch how it continually flows and never runs dry. Let it remind you of the living water Jesus offers.
- Carry a "guaranteed fire" reminder by putting a disposable lighter in your pocket this week to remind yourself to go to God first.
- Simplify your gear by removing redundant or unreliable items from your pack. Let this act of stripping away represent removing worldly distractions from your spiritual life.
- Memorize John 4:14 on an outdoor solitude walk and repeat it aloud when you feel tempted to chase fulfillment anywhere but in Christ.

WILD DESTINATION

Imagine planning for a once-in-a-lifetime camping and hiking trip.

You spend months getting into shape. You train by walking trails with a loaded pack, breaking in boots, and testing trekking poles. You methodically sift through your camping gear and weed out anything unnecessary. You take online courses on backcountry skills, buy a whole new wardrobe just for the experience, and spend hours reading blogs and watching videos from seasoned hikers.

You research the best meals for weight and nutrition. You test out your new ultralight tent. You hop into online forums, ask questions, and share your excitement with fellow adventure-lovers. You practice filtering creek water and even rehearse your nighttime bathroom routine in the woods.

You plan out every ounce in your pack by cutting the handle off your toothbrush, swapping heavy stuff sacks for lighter ones, and making sure you're absolutely dialed in.

And then the big day comes.

You pack the car, slide into the front seat, and open your map app. Then it hits you.

You forgot to choose the destination.

You've planned every single detail of the journey, except *where you're going.*

This sounds ridiculous, right? No one in their right mind would spend so much time, effort, and energy on the trip of a lifetime without ever deciding where it was supposed to end. And yet I did exactly that. And I'm not alone.

I spent the first twenty years of my adult life preparing, planning, and organizing everything, including my business, my career, my image, my goals, and my finances. But I never really considered the final destination.

Everything I did was focused on temporary things, such as career goals, possessions, recognition, income, and accolades. But I was like a man with a packed bag and nowhere to go. I had prepared for a journey, but not the *right* journey.

One day in my early forties, I realized I had never actually mapped my life toward *eternity.* I was navigating a million trails but never stopped to consider where they would ultimately lead. I was chasing temporary rewards with eternal energy.

It's easy to get tangled up in the plans of life. It's so easy to pour our time, effort, money, and mental energy into things that have nothing to do with the eternal destination God created us for. Many are experts at planning the journey but often forget to begin with the end in mind.

As Hebrews 12:1–2 reminds us, "Therefore, since we are surrounded by such a great cloud of witnesses, let us throw off everything that hinders and the sin that so easily entangles. And let us run with perseverance the race marked out for us, fixing our eyes on Jesus, the pioneer and perfecter of faith." When we don't start with eternity as our destination, and Jesus as our navigator, our lives become filled with things that hinder. We carry burdens we were never meant to carry. We say yes to every opportunity without asking, "Is this leading me closer to Christ?" We wander with full packs and no direction.

The problem isn't in the *planning*, it's in *what* we're planning for.

Paul gives us a course correction in 2 Corinthians 4:18: "So we fix our eyes not on what is seen, but on what is unseen, since what is seen is temporary, but what is unseen is eternal."

The unseen is the eternal. It is the heart and soul. It's the relationship we cultivate with the Lord. The destination we're meant for is eternity with Him. And getting there requires more than busy hands or a full pack; it requires a surrendered heart. Colossians 3:1–2 says it like this: "Since, then, you have been raised with Christ, set your hearts on things above, where Christ is, seated at the right hand of God. Set your minds on things above, not on earthly things."

This shift doesn't come naturally. It's hard to focus on the invisible when the visible screams for our attention at every turn. It takes faith to plan your life for a place you've never seen and to live each day with eternity in mind. But the Lord promises that He knows the way and that He can be trusted with your route. He reminds us of this in Jeremiah 29:11: "'For I know the plans I have for you,' declares the Lord, 'plans to prosper you and not to harm you, plans to give you hope and a future.'"

God isn't asking you to plan your own destination, He's already prepared it. He's just asking you to trust Him enough to walk the path He's mapped out for you toward it.

So let me ask you . . .

Have you chosen a destination?

Or are you still planning your trip without deciding where you want to end up?

Your car is packed. The map app is open. And the Lord is whispering the coordinates.

Where do you really want to go?

IN THE WILD

Verse to Contemplate

> I press on toward the goal to win the prize for which God has called me heavenward in Christ Jesus. (Phil. 3:14)

QUESTIONS FOR THE WILDERNESS JOURNAL

1. If someone looked at your time, money, and energy, what destination would they think you're aiming for?
2. Are you planning your life around what is seen or what is unseen?
3. What's one area of your life that's packed and prepped but may not be pointing toward eternity?
4. What might it look like for you to "set your heart on things above" this week?
5. Are you more focused on the gear or the goal?

PRAYER OF THE DAY

Lord, I don't want to be packed for the wrong destination. Fix my eyes on You, both my compass and goal. Help me release the temporary plans and distractions that weigh me down. Refocus my energy on what truly matters: the unseen things of Your kingdom. Teach me to walk each day with eternity in mind, trusting that You know the plans You have for me. I surrender the map. I surrender the trail. I choose to follow You. In Jesus's name, amen.

WILDERNESS APPLICATION

- Draw a timeline "life map" in your journal—birth to eternity. Add spiritual milestones and places where you took wrong turns. Pray over where God wants to lead you next.
- Go on a short hike with no set trail. Stop at three to five points to pray for direction, clarity, and surrender for different areas of your life.
- Lay out something you've been striving for (e.g., a project, plan, or possession). Ask: Is this helping me reach my real destination or weighing me down?
- Write Colossians 3:1–2 or 2 Corinthians 4:18 on an index card and place it where you'll see it daily, such as your steering wheel, your mirror, or your backpack.
- Take a hike and write a personal mission statement that starts with "My final destination is eternity with Jesus. Therefore, I will . . ."

WILD EXTENDER

When I teach my fire starting classes, I always start by teaching students how to ignite the perfect fire tinder, a cotton ball. The natural seed pod of cotton, what we know as a cotton ball in modern society, is the perfect fire tinder. It's made up of small, flammable fibers, it's dry, and it easily ignites with just a spark.

However, even though cotton is the perfect fire tinder, one cotton ball will burn only a few seconds. In a real survival situation, especially in cold weather or rainy conditions, one to two seconds of burn time, even from perfect tinder like cotton, doesn't give a survivor much of a chance to get a fire started.

After teaching this principle, I then ask my students to mix a dollop of petroleum jelly into the fibers of a cotton ball. This fuel, known as a flame extender, turns the cotton into a wick. When a flame extender is mixed with the fibers, one cotton ball can burn as long as ten minutes. It is a dramatic demonstration.

There are numerous flame extenders that can be used in a survival situation: petroleum jelly, wax, and even pine or spruce resin. A flame extender does just what the phrase suggests: It makes the tinder burn longer, stronger, and brighter. Adding a flame extender to a dry tinder such as the fluffy seed pod from a cotton plant gives someone a much higher chance of success in getting a fire started, even in extreme conditions.

Below are some very practical, improvised tinder and flame extender combinations that could potentially save your life one day:

- cotton ball mixed with petroleum jelly
- cattail fluff mixed with lip balm
- milkweed down mixed with wax from a candle
- the fluffy seed head of the goldenrod plant mixed with the sticky resin from a pine tree
- dried grasses mixed with flammable spruce resin

If only there was something, a spiritual extender, that could be added to our faith to make it burn stronger, longer, and more brightly, just like in the case of fire starting.

There is.

It's called obedience.

Obedience is to faith what petroleum jelly is to a cotton ball. It turns a short-lived spiritual spark into a long-burning flame. When we are obedient, not just to God's commands but to His voice, His nudges, and His leading in our daily lives, we begin to see Him respond to our obedience. When we see that response and experience the results of our obedience, our faith increases. That deeper faith helps us be more obedient next time, because we trust Him more. That's the compounding nature of faith. The more obedient we are, the more faithful we become, and the more our faith grows.

Obedience is an extender.

And Scripture is filled with affirmations of this very principle. Take James 2:22, for example: "You see that his faith and his actions were working together, and his faith was made complete by what he did." Faith and obedience go hand in hand. Just like fire and fuel, they rely on each other. Faith isn't fully formed until it's acted upon, and when it is, it's strengthened. Then there's John 14:21: "Whoever has my commands and keeps them is the one who loves me. The one who loves me will be loved by my Father, and I too will love them and show myself to them." Jesus promises that when we obey, He will show Himself to us. Obedience leads to encounters like the one I wrote about in the devotional titled "Wild Encounter" (p. 138). When we see God move in response to our obedience, it grows our trust in Him, and that deepens our faith. We can't talk about trust and not learn from what happened to Abraham in Genesis 22. Abraham raised a knife to sacrifice his son Isaac, and the Lord intervened.

> Then he reached out his hand and took the knife to slay his son. But the angel of the LORD called out to him from heaven, "Abraham! Abraham!"
>
> "Here I am," he replied.
>
> "Do not lay a hand on the boy," he said. "Do not do anything to him. Now I know that you fear God, because you have not withheld from me your son, your only son." (vv. 10–12)

Abraham's faith was active: He obeyed before he fully understood the outcome. His obedience opened the door for God's promise to be fulfilled. Later, God confirmed His blessing in Genesis 22:16–18: "I swear by myself, declares the LORD, that because you have done this and have not withheld your son, your only son, I will surely bless you and make your descendants as numerous as the stars in the sky and as the sand on the seashore. Your descendants will take possession of the cities of their enemies, and through your offspring all nations on earth will be blessed, because you have obeyed me."

Abraham is a perfect example that faith isn't a feeling, it's action. Obedience activates and strengthens faith, even before we see the outcome. Obedience comes from faith, but it also feeds it. The more we obey, the more our confidence in God grows. Each step of obedience builds another layer of trust. God's responses are affirmations that He sees you, knows you, and is with you. This is where extending the flame of faith really happens!

IN THE WILD

Verse to Contemplate

> You see that his faith and his actions were working together, and his faith was made complete by what he did. (James 2:22)

QUESTIONS FOR THE WILDERNESS JOURNAL

1. Where is God asking you to be obedient right now, even in something small?
2. Can you recall a moment when your obedience clearly ignited a deeper level of faith?

3. What areas of your faith feel like a spark waiting for fuel?
4. How might your daily routines change if obedience became your first response to God's voice?
5. What flame has nearly gone out in your life because it lacked obedience to sustain it?

PRAYER OF THE DAY

Father, thank You for the spark of faith You've placed in my heart. I don't want it to burn out. I want it to grow. Teach me to mix obedience with faith like fuel to a fire starter. Help me trust You enough to act when You speak, and let my obedience be the fuel that keeps the fire alive. Strengthen me through each small yes and let my life burn brightly for Your glory. In Jesus's name, amen.

WILDERNESS APPLICATION

- Go outside and build two fire bundles, one made of plain tinder and the other treated with a flame extender like petroleum jelly or pine resin. Light both and watch the difference. As the longer-burning bundle glows, reflect on what obedience adds to your spiritual fire.
- Write a short prayer in your journal asking God to help you obey Him in one specific area this week.

- Carry a cotton ball in your pocket or bag this week as a physical reminder that obedience keeps your faith burning.
- Share a story with someone else about a time when obedience changed the course of your life or deepened your trust in God.

WILD RIVER

I'll never forget filming an episode of *SOS: How to Survive* for The Weather Channel in Kern, California. In that episode, I was demonstrating how to build an improvised flotation device using a backpack. This is something you might need to survive if you're caught in rising floodwaters. The river we chose for the demonstration was the Kern River, swollen with spring rain and snowmelt. It was wild, unpredictable, and fast.

Our filming plan was simple: capture multiple angles of me floating down the same stretch of river, showing how to stay afloat and steer through rapids. I'd get in at one spot, float down through the rapids, and get out at the same spot every time. Consistency was important for the filming process.

But something unexpected began to happen.

Each time I got in the river, even though it was the same stretch, the experience was completely different. One time a massive log drifted up behind me. Another time I was pulled toward boulders I hadn't encountered before. On a different take, I was sucked into a fast-moving current and nearly missed the safety crew waiting downstream.

Despite me entering the same exact river in the same exact spot, the path was never the same. The water was never the same. The dangers and obstacles were never the same. The entrance and exit were the same, but that was it. The entire journey each time was different.

The Kern River was alive, always moving, shifting, adapting, and flowing. Its power humbled me as it took me on the journey it wanted, regardless of what our film crew had planned.

Strangely enough, I have the same experience when I open up the Word of God.

There are passages I've read dozens of times, sometimes even in the same location. Often, they are underlined and familiar. But depending on where I'm at in life, it speaks to me in a completely new way. It convicts in a new area. It comforts a new wound. It brings courage to a new fear.

It's as if the same river of God's truth flows in a new way every time I step in, even if it's the exact spot I've stepped in before. Hebrews 4:12 gives us insight into this feeling: "For the word of God is alive and active. Sharper than any double-edged sword, it penetrates even to dividing soul and spirit, joints and marrow; it judges the thoughts and attitudes of the heart."

The Bible isn't just ink on paper. It's a wild river of living truth that flows straight from the heart of God. And it meets you differently depending on what's floating in your life at that moment. What's more, God knows exactly how and when to let His Word reach you. Isaiah writes, "The Sovereign Lord has given me a well-instructed tongue, to know the word that sustains the weary. He wakens me morning by morning, wakens my ear to listen like one being instructed" (50:4).

No matter where your feet are in life or what path you're on, the Word of God is designed to speak to it. Even when two people read the same exact verse, God speaks through His living Word in unique, individualized, and deeply personal ways. One verse can give comfort to the grieving, guidance to the lost, and instruction to the searching, all at once. And we're not in this alone. John 14:26 says: "But the Helper, the Holy Spirit, whom the Father will send in My name, He will teach you all things, and bring to your remembrance all things that I said to you" (ESV).

God's Word speaks directly to us through the Holy Spirit. Jesus left the Holy Spirit behind to dwell within us and to guide us into truth and help us understand the Scriptures. Sometimes, reading the same passage can feel like reading something entirely new. Not because the words have changed but because we have. And the Holy Spirit knows exactly what our hearts need to hear in each moment.

Same Word.

Same river of truth.

Different need.

Different experience.

IN THE WILD

Verse to Contemplate

> For the word of God is alive and active. Sharper than any double-edged sword, it penetrates even to dividing soul and spirit, joints and marrow; it judges the thoughts and attitudes of the heart. (Heb. 4:12)

QUESTIONS FOR THE WILDERNESS JOURNAL

1. Have you experienced a moment when a familiar verse hit you differently than it ever had before?
2. What are you walking through right now that the Word of God might speak directly into?
3. Are you allowing Scripture to shape your journey or are you just floating through it?
4. What spiritual currents are pulling you right now? Are you resisting the Word, or surrendering to it?
5. How does the idea of Scripture as a living, flowing river change the way you approach Bible reading?

PRAYER OF THE DAY

Father, thank You for Your Word that moves, flows, and lives. Thank You that it's not a dead text but a living current that meets me exactly where I am. Teach me to come to it expectantly, ready to hear whatever You want to say today. Let Your Word rush through the dry places in my life, and guide me through every rapid, every bend, and every moment I feel lost. In Jesus's name, amen.

WILDERNESS APPLICATION

Go outside and find a body of moving water such as a creek, stream, or river, if possible. Sit by the edge and open your Bible to a passage you've read before. As you listen to the water move, ask the Holy Spirit to speak through the familiar words in a fresh way. Watch how the current shifts and flows and remember that so does God's Word. It's the same passage, but a new moment. Let it guide you.

WILD RULES OF THREE

I can't tell you how many times I've seen someone in one of my survival courses raise their hand and say that food is their number one survival priority and that skills such as hunting, fishing, and trapping wild game are the most important. But the truth is, in almost every emergency survival situation, food is far from the top of the list.

In survival, we often use a phrase called the rule of threes to help us stay focused when everything around us is falling apart. It goes like this: In extreme conditions, you can't live more than three hours without shelter, three days without water, or three weeks without food.

Shelter comes first because keeping your core body temperature regulated is often the difference between life and death. Water is next because proper hydration impacts nearly every bodily function. Then, and only then, does food become a concern. Fire plays a crucial role in all three. It keeps you warm, boils your water, cooks your food, helps with signaling, and even provides comfort when you're alone in the wilderness.

When you're in a survival situation, you have to put the first thing first. There's no time or energy to waste. Get that wrong, and it might be your last mistake.

This same principle reminds me of something Jesus modeled in His own life. In Mark 1:35, we catch a glimpse of a pivotal moment early in His ministry: "Very early in the morning, while it was still dark, Jesus got up, left the house and went off to a solitary place, where he prayed."

Just the night before, Jesus had taught in the synagogue, healed the sick, and cast out demons. The Bible says the entire town had gathered at His door. He was in demand, to say the least. But the next morning, while it was still dark, Jesus got up, left the house, and went to a solitary place, most likely a wilderness area, to pray. As we learn in Mark 1:36–39, even his disciples seemed a little perplexed by Jesus's behavior:

> Simon and his companions went to look for him, and when they found him, they exclaimed: "Everyone is looking for you!"
>
> Jesus replied, "Let us go somewhere else—to the nearby villages—so I can preach there also. That is why I have come." So he traveled throughout Galilee, preaching in their synagogues and driving out demons.

Even though He was being sought out by crowds, even though His disciples came looking for Him with urgent needs, even though He was the Son of God with the power to do everything they asked of Him, Jesus put the first thing first.

He prioritized solitude with the Father and the Holy Spirit. Prayer was His spiritual shelter. It was His reset and His source of power and clarity in a chaotic, distracting, and demanding world. Solitude was the flame that kept everything else ablaze.

If Jesus, who was entirely God and entirely human, needed to withdraw and spend time with the Father to start His day, how much more do we?

So many mornings, it's easy to wake up and jump straight into your to-do list of checking emails, starting chores, and scrolling through headlines. But in both survival and faith, your ability to endure often comes down to one simple principle: You must put the first thing first. Like Jesus, start your day by seeking shelter in the presence of the Father. Let prayer be your covering. Let His Word be your living water. Let the fire of the Holy Spirit prepare and sustain you for whatever lies ahead. When you begin your day grounded in Him, everything else can fall into place.

IN THE WILD

Verse to Contemplate

> Very early in the morning, while it was still dark, Jesus got up, left the house and went off to a solitary place, where He prayed. (Mark 1:35)

QUESTIONS FOR THE WILDERNESS JOURNAL

1. What typically grabs your attention first each day? Is it emails, noise, tasks, or time with God?
2. Have you ever experienced a kind of spiritual hypothermia that entails drifting from God's warmth and protection because of misplaced priorities?

3. What does shelter in God's presence practically look like for you?
4. How can you recenter your morning routine around spiritual survival priorities?
5. What would it look like for you to treat prayer and Scripture like fire, shelter, and water for your soul?

PRAYER OF THE DAY

Father, thank You for being my first shelter, my first water, and the fire that sustains me. Forgive me for the times I've rushed into my day without anchoring myself in You. Teach me to put the first thing first and to seek Your face before I seek anything else. Let every day begin with Your presence as my foundation. In Jesus's name, amen.

WILDERNESS APPLICATION

Build a simple spiritual survival kit for your mornings. Choose three items: a Bible, a journal, and a dedicated outdoor spot. Each morning this week, commit to spending ten minutes outside with God before anything else. Like firewood gathered before the storm, stock your soul with warmth, wisdom, and direction. Let this rhythm become your rule of spiritual survival—three things before anything else: solitude, Scripture, and surrender.

WILD STORM

In an earlier devotional, I talked about how I had a business of selling T-shirts at fairs and festivals to make ends meet while starting my survival business. I'd live out of my truck, setting up a booth by day and camping at state parks or festival grounds by night. After one such summer event in Florida, I finally decided to check something off my personal bucket list: camping on the beach. I drove to the coast, pitched my tent right on the sand, and settled in for what I thought would be a dreamlike night under the stars.

But in my excitement, despite being a survival instructor, I forgot one of the most basic rules of trip planning: Check the weather.

What started as a perfect, peaceful afternoon turned into one of the worst storms I've ever witnessed. The winds howled, the tent collapsed repeatedly onto my head, and I realized I hadn't even staked it down. I was the only thing keeping it grounded. Fearing things would only get worse, I grabbed what I could, unzipped the front flap, and sprinted toward my truck a couple hundred yards away. As I turned around, I watched my tent lift into the air and disappear into the storm, taking all my gear with it.

Looking back at that night when I was soaked and shivering, I think that is what the disciples must have felt in Mark 4:35–41:

> That day when evening came, he said to his disciples, "Let us go over to the other side." Leaving the crowd behind, they took him along, just as he was, in the boat. There were also other boats with him. A furious squall came up, and the waves broke over the boat, so that it was nearly swamped. Jesus was in the stern, sleeping on a cushion. The disciples woke him and said to him, "Teacher, don't you care if we drown?"
>
> He got up, rebuked the wind and said to the waves, "Quiet! Be still!" Then the wind died down and it was completely calm.
>
> He said to his disciples, "Why are you so afraid? Do you still have no faith?"
>
> They were terrified and asked each other, "Who is this? Even the wind and the waves obey him!"

What strikes me most about that story is that Jesus allowed the storm—and the disciples' anxiety—to build to the breaking point before He stepped in. I believe that moment wasn't just a miracle; it was a living parable. One they would never forget.

Storms like that leave a mark. That storm in Florida left a mark on me. But years later, I faced another storm. This time, the storm wasn't outside in the weather, it was inside of me.

At around 1:30 a.m. one night, I shot awake with a racing heart, nausea, dizziness, and shortness of breath. I was sweating through my sheets. It felt like a nine-hundred-pound gorilla was sitting on my chest. Convinced I was having a heart attack,

I jumped in the car and headed to the ER, with my wife on the phone praying I'd make it.

But tests showed nothing wrong with my heart. It had been a panic attack.

Storms take many forms. Some rage outside us. Some rage within. But Jesus brings literal peace in the middle of chaos. Not just to wind and waves like on the boat with His disciples but to fear, anxiety, and trauma.

Jesus promises a calm to the storm. And this is a peace rooted not in circumstance but in Christ Himself: "Peace I leave with you; my peace I give you. I do not give to you as the world gives. Do not let your hearts be troubled and do not be afraid" (John 14:27).

Before Jesus stood up in the boat, the disciples were locked onto the storm. But when He spoke to the storm with authority, their focus shifted. And that's the key. Peace doesn't come from pretending there's no storm. It comes from fixing our eyes on the One who commands it. But, as Paul writes to the Philippians, this kind of peace is something we pursue through trust, prayer, and surrender. It's a focus shift: "Do not be anxious about anything, but in every situation, by prayer and petition, with thanksgiving, present your requests to God. And the peace of God, which transcends all understanding, will guard your hearts and your minds in Christ Jesus" (4:6–7).

When we shift our focus to Jesus, even the wildest storm can't shake our peace.

IN THE WILD

Verse to Contemplate

He got up, rebuked the wind and said to the waves, "Quiet! Be still!" Then the wind died down and it was completely calm. (Mark 4:39)

QUESTIONS FOR THE WILDERNESS JOURNAL

1. What storm are you facing right now, externally or internally?
2. Are you trying to control the storm, escape it, or surrender it to Jesus?
3. What would it look like to fix your eyes on the Savior instead of the storm?
4. Have you experienced the peace of Christ even when your circumstances didn't change?

PRAYER OF THE DAY

Jesus, You are Lord over every storm, both within me and around me. I confess how often I focus on the wind and waves instead of You. Help me shift my eyes from the chaos to Your calm. Teach me to trust in Your timing, rest in Your presence, and cling to Your peace. Guard my heart and mind as I surrender this storm to You. In Your name, amen.

WILDERNESS APPLICATION

Build a small campfire or sit quietly by an existing one. Let the flames remind you of Jesus's steady presence. As you sit, identify one storm that's weighing on you. It can be physical, emotional, or spiritual. Imagine handing it over to Him. Read Mark 4:39 aloud and let the fire become your visual reminder of His peace. As the flames dance, whisper your storm to God and ask Him to calm your soul like He calmed the sea. Return to this moment whenever the storm tries to rise again.

WILD CUT

There's a certain kind of embarrassment that cuts deeper than words. I can still feel it today.

Early in my career, I was featured on a regional morning news show in Chicago because my survival school had just been named one of the top ten in the world. I was in my early twenties, with more confidence than actual experience, and I saw this as a big opportunity to fill some courses. I showed up ready to prove myself with a live demonstration of one of the hardest primitive fire starting techniques: the bow drill.

I was calm on the outside, but inside I was buzzing with nerves. This was my big moment, and my skills would be on display in front of hundreds of thousands of people. After a few minutes of banter with the show host, the time had come.

The smoke came fast as I began spinning, but the ember never formed. I pushed harder, faster. My heart pounded as I noticed the giant countdown clock on the wall—thirty seconds left. I doubled down with everything I had. No ember.

Five seconds.

Four.

Three.

Two.

One.

Then, live on the air, the host said, "Well, it doesn't look like Creek is going to be able to start a fire today. But maybe you'll have better luck in one of his classes."

Cue the ending jingle. Camera off. Segment over.

There I knelt, sweaty, embarrassed, and crushed. I'd failed on live television in front of hundreds of thousands. And worst of all, there were no do-overs. I'd been given one shot, and I blew it.

My career didn't end there, but my pride sure took a hit. That moment marked me, and I wished for a redo I would never get.

Have you ever desperately wanted a second chance?

Maybe it wasn't in front of a camera, but maybe it was in front of your kids. Or your spouse. Maybe it was a choice you made that you'd give anything to take back. Or something you should have said but didn't. The origin for the desire for a second chance takes many forms.

I think of King David in Psalm 51. His moment was far worse than mine. After committing adultery with Bathsheba and arranging her husband's death, the cat is suddenly out of the bag. There's no hiding. No spin. Just raw, broken repentance.

> Create in me a pure heart, O God,
> and renew a steadfast spirit within me.
> Do not cast me from your presence
> or take your Holy Spirit from me.
> Restore to me the joy of your salvation
> and grant me a willing spirit, to sustain me. (vv. 10–12)

David pleads for a second chance. His goal is not to escape the consequences but to be restored. He desires renewal and forgiveness.

The good news for us is that God is the God of second chances. In fact, He's the God of seventy-times-seven chances, as we're reminded in Matthew 18:21–22: "Then Peter came to Jesus and asked, 'Lord, how many times shall I forgive my brother or sister who sins against me? Up to seven times?' Jesus answered, 'I tell you, not seven times, but seventy-seven times.'"

He doesn't just give us another shot, He offers new life. That second chance in life we all long for is found in Jesus Christ. Through His sacrifice on the cross, we aren't just patched up, we're made new. The slate isn't just wiped clean, it's replaced with His righteousness. Surrender to Him means that when God looks at us, He sees Jesus instead. Galatians 2:20 puts it this way: "I have been crucified with Christ and I no longer live, but Christ lives in me. The life I now live in the body, I live by faith in the Son of God, who loved me and gave himself for me."

Scripture is filled with iterations of this truth. I think God knew how many times we'd need to hear it to believe it. Below are just two more affirmations:

> In him we have redemption through his blood, the forgiveness of sins, in accordance with the riches of God's grace. (Eph. 1:7)

> But God demonstrates his own love for us in this: While we were still sinners, Christ died for us. (Rom. 5:8)

Another great example of second chances is when Jesus looked at the woman caught in adultery. The crowd wanted judgment, but He offered mercy.

> Jesus straightened up and asked her, "Woman, where are they? Has no one condemned you?"
>
> "No one, sir," she said.
>
> "Then neither do I condemn you," Jesus declared. "Go now and leave your life of sin." (John 8:10–11)

But notice how Jesus wants that second chance to begin. It must be a 180-degree turn from sin. It's a new direction, with sin left in the distance. A second chance is a wild cut through the wilderness of shame and regret, back to grace and purpose.

IN THE WILD

Verse to Contemplate

> Create in me a pure heart, O God,
> and renew a steadfast spirit within me.
> (Ps. 51:10)

QUESTIONS FOR THE WILDERNESS JOURNAL

1. When have you felt the sting of failure or embarrassment and longed for a second chance?
2. What is one moment in your life you need to lay at the feet of Jesus today?
3. How might you extend the same grace you've received to someone else this week?

PRAYER OF THE DAY

Lord, I've failed more times than I can count. But You are faithful and full of mercy. Thank You for not giving up on me, for cutting through my shame with the truth of Your love. Create in me a clean heart, renew my spirit, and lead me on. I receive Your grace and surrender my past. Thank You for the second chance I find in Jesus. Amen.

WILDERNESS APPLICATION

Find a patch of raw earth or dirt. Kneel down and use a stick to write a failure or regret in the dirt, something you've been carrying. Now, smooth over the dirt with your hand until the words disappear. Say out loud, "In Christ, I am made new." Now, draw a cross. This represents where your second chance was written in blood and sealed forever.

WILD ULU

I have a personal motto when it comes to knives: You can never have too many. This love for blades is rooted in fond memories of carving with my grandpa on the farm when I was a boy. My appreciation for a good knife and the skill that goes into making one grew stronger and stronger as my knife skills developed in my survival training business. In survival training, nearly everything revolves around a cutting tool of some kind.

I'll never forget seeing an ulu being used for the first time. I was in Alaska and had the privilege of watching an Inuit woman demonstrate how to fillet a king salmon in a traditional way for hanging using an ulu. I stood in awe as she masterfully processed, deboned, filleted, and cut the salmon for hanging on a wooden smoking rack. It was an amazing display of not only her skill but of the functionality of the ulu. Years later, after filming a survival television show in Canada, the production crew gifted me my first ulu, and I eagerly added it to my tool chest of blades.

The ulu is a traditional all-purpose knife used by the Inuit, Yupik, and Aleut peoples of the Arctic. Its name means "woman's knife" in some Inuit dialects, and it has been handed down for generations. Typically, it features a broad, curved blade with a handle mounted above the blade, allowing for a rocking motion when cutting. Historically, it was used for everything from skinning animals and filleting fish to preparing food and cutting snow blocks for igloos. Its design reflects centuries of innovation, practicality, and adaptation to the arctic environment, demonstrating how a tool can be perfectly suited to the tasks it was created to perform. The ulu is more than a knife; it is a cultural emblem, connecting generations and sustaining communities through skill, patience, and care.

As I watched the Inuit woman use the ulu, it struck me how different the tool was compared to the knives I grew up using. Other than being made from metal, there were no similarities at all. Yet it was arguably one of the most functional knives I've ever seen wielded, and I left that demonstration with a great deal of respect for not only the uniqueness of the knife itself but also the display of skill by the Inuit woman. She used the knife she knew and grew up with, just as I used the knife I knew and grew up with. Though totally different, they served the same purpose.

Just as a blade can be small, unusual, or even imperfect yet perfectly effective, our lives, though diverse, scarred, or seemingly limited, can accomplish exactly what God designed them for. In the wilderness, I've seen it time and again: A small knife, a makeshift tool, or a skillful adaptation can save a life, build a shelter, or start a fire when it's needed most.

So it is with God and your unique design. Your experiences, your limitations, and even your past struggles are tools, not barriers. God can use them to accomplish His purposes.

In the same way I stood in awe of the Inuit woman and her ulu, I love watching people use what God has given them for kingdom work. If I'm being honest, I have to fight feelings of jealousy sometimes when I see a great spiritual gift, such as leading praise and worship, on display. But 1 Corinthians 12:4–6 reminds us that, though each person has different gifts, the Lord remains the same throughout: "There are different kinds of gifts, but the same Spirit distributes them. There are different kinds of service, but the same Lord. There are different kinds of working, but in all of them and in everyone it is the same God at work."

God's calling is relational and situational, not formulaic. He doesn't call everyone to the same tasks, the same paths, or the same tools. He calls each of us to step into the place where He has already put us and to use what He has already given us.

This truth applies not only to spiritual gifts but also to our past experiences, passions, and unique abilities or disabilities. Each of us is uniquely different, and all these differences are useful to God. After surrendering my life to Christ fully in my early forties, I remember asking the Lord, "What am I supposed to do now? I'm not a preacher or a missionary. I'm a wilderness survival instructor." I'll never forget His clear response: "I want you to be exactly who I've made you to be. Use where I've put you, with the gifts, talents, experiences, and abilities I've given you, for My glory and to share the hope and love that Jesus offers the world."

I didn't change my profession, but I did change my perspective. My past, my skills, and even my failures became tools God could use, and my life took on new purpose. I still teach wilderness survival skills, but now I do it to honor and bring glory to God.

One of the most inspiring examples of someone using their unique form for God's glory is Nick Vujicic. Nick was born in Melbourne, Australia, with a disorder called tetra-amelia, which causes the very rare absence of all four limbs. Despite severe limitations, he can write, swim, and even play some sports using adapted methods. But what's truly inspirational is that he has turned his condition into a platform for sharing the gospel through speaking engagements and a ministry he founded called Life Without Limbs. Talk about a human ulu!

With Christ, there is incredible unity in diversity. First Corinthians 12:12 reminds us, "Just as a body, though one, has many parts, but all its many parts form one body, so it is with Christ."

Ephesians 4:16 is another powerful reminder that embracing each of our unique designs and circumstances strengthens the whole: "From him the whole body, joined and held together by every supporting ligament, grows and builds itself up in love, as each part does its work."

God can use everything about you, including your skills, your passions, your past, your experiences, and even your limitations, to point others to Him. Like the ulu, your life may look different from someone else's, but it can accomplish exactly what it was designed to do. God doesn't ask you to be someone else. He doesn't call you to use gifts you don't have. But He does invite you to examine your life, your experiences, your talents, and even your limitations, and ask, "Lord, how can You use this for Your glory?"

Like a skilled craftsman shaping a blade, God can take what you already have and transform it into something that serves

His purposes. Your life, in its uniqueness, can point to His greatness, just like the ulu points to the skill, wisdom, and culture of generations past.

IN THE WILD

Verses to Contemplate

> There are different kinds of gifts, but the same Spirit distributes them. There are different kinds of service, but the same Lord. There are different kinds of working, but in all of them and in everyone it is the same God at work. (1 Cor. 12:4–6)

QUESTIONS FOR THE WILDERNESS JOURNAL

1. What gifts, talents, experiences, or struggles has God placed in your life that you've overlooked or dismissed?
2. How can you view your limitations and past experiences as tools, not barriers?
3. Are there ways God is calling you to use what He has given you for His glory?

PRAYER OF THE DAY

Lord, thank You for the life You've given me, including my gifts, experiences, and even my limitations. Help me see that nothing is wasted and teach me to use all You've placed in my life with purpose, like a skilled craftsman wields a blade. Give me courage to embrace my uniqueness, to trust Your design, and to ask daily, "Lord, how can You use this?" May my life, in all its differences and imperfections, point to You and bring glory to Your name. In Jesus's name, amen.

WILDERNESS APPLICATION

- Take a quiet moment outdoors and write down your unique skills, experiences, and even challenges. Ask God to show you how He can use each one.
- Think of a time in the wilderness when an unexpected tool or skill saved the day. How does this reflect how God might use unexpected parts of your life?
- This week, choose one tool from your life, such as a skill, passion, experience, or even a challenge, and intentionally use it to bless someone or point them toward God.

WILD FRUIT

As I've mentioned before, when I taught my first survival class, I knew little more than what I'd learned earning the wilderness survival merit badge in Boy Scouts. It became obvious very quickly that I was not an expert on the subject. I knew I needed to spend a lot of time studying, training, and learning more to achieve even a respectable level of competence in teaching survival skills.

For over two decades, I've strived to be the best survival and preparedness instructor possible. I've read countless manuals, spoken with and interviewed people more knowledgeable than myself, and invested thousands of hours training in the field. I poured my heart and soul into becoming proficient in my skill sets. After many years of hard work, I finally began to feel confident in my ability to not only make good survival decisions but also teach others to do the same.

I remember when news outlets started calling me a survival expert. I'll never be entirely comfortable with that term, but I worked incredibly hard for it.

Whether you're a survival instructor, musician, athlete, author, or anything else, it's foolish to think you can excel without discipline, training, commitment, and passion. We all know that being good at something requires consistent effort.

This is true in all areas of life, including faith.

Just a few short years ago, I wasn't doing life well. I didn't have the peace I wanted or the joy I felt I deserved. I felt far from God, and my relationship with Jesus was on the level of a distant pen pal, at best. My relationships with family and friends were also suffering.

The bottom line is that I wasn't bearing fruit like Jesus described in John 15:8: "This is to my Father's glory, that you bear much fruit, showing yourselves to be my disciples."

Fruit is the obvious result of a life grounded in Christlikeness. We all want to bear fruit.

It's crazy that I could understand I needed to invest countless hours training to be a good survival instructor but somehow believed I could produce good spiritual fruit without investing any time, effort, or energy into knowing Jesus and becoming more like Him.

I guess I thought that as long as I occasionally went to church and prayed before meals, I'd magically wake up one day and be an expert in living a Christlike life. Well, as you can imagine, that plan didn't work out too well.

Instead of the fruits I wanted, my harvest was filled with anxiety, impatience, and selfishness. I was frustrated that my spiritual expertise was nonexistent, even though I was exercising virtually no self-discipline in seeking a deeper understanding of what it means to live in Christ.

I wanted the good fruit and knew it was going to take effort to get it.

So, just as I had sought to become a survival expert, I pursued the discipline needed to develop my spiritual skill set. With Jesus as my mentor, I began to train the way He did. His disciplines included solitude, simplicity, study, prayer, service, and fasting. He practiced these to draw closer to the Father and stay focused. They also helped Him keep free from distractions.

Just as these disciplines were not optional for Him, they couldn't be optional for me.

Paul even discusses this in 1 Corinthians 9:24–27:

> Do you not know that in a race all the runners run, but only one gets the prize? Run in such a way as to get the prize. Everyone who competes in the games goes into strict training. They do it to get a crown that will not last, but we do it to get a crown that will last forever.
>
> Therefore I do not run like someone running aimlessly; I do not fight like a boxer beating the air. No, I strike a blow to my body and make it my slave so that after I have preached to others, I myself will not be disqualified for the prize.

The goal was to use these disciplines to be as obedient as possible to the greatest commandment: "Love the Lord your God with all your heart and with all your soul and with all your mind and with all your strength" (Mark 12:30).

I'm still very much on this journey, but I've made a concerted effort to replace some of my old habits with these new disciplines. I'm trying my best to make my relationship with Jesus part of every aspect of every day, rather than just an occasional

Sunday morning or a routine mealtime prayer like "God is good. God is great. Thank You for this food. Amen."

I know this journey will never truly end, and the more I learn about God and about myself through Him, the more I realize how much I still have to learn. I'll never master this skill, but I'll keep trying as long as I live!

I can report that investing in my spiritual life has undoubtedly better prepared me to survive the temptations and challenges life throws my way. With discipline, I can apply the truths of Scripture to my daily life to best honor God with my actions and decisions.

In much the same way that storing food and water prepares us for uncertain times, spiritual discipline equips us to respond to life's curveballs in a Christlike manner. And just like with mastering the bow drill, there are no shortcuts.

You have to do the work if you want the reward. The reward is a life filled with love, joy, peace, forbearance, kindness, goodness, faithfulness, gentleness, and self-control. The bonus is that this good fruit comes regardless of whether things are going well or not. Bad stuff happens to all of us, but God is always good, no matter our circumstances. His promise in James 1:12 remains true even in the trials: "Blessed is the one who perseveres under trial because, having stood the test, that person will receive the crown of life that the Lord has promised to those who love him."

If you're not happy with your fruit harvest right now, maybe it's time to take the idea of spiritual disciplines seriously. Nothing is going to change (for the better) without it.

IN THE WILD

Verses to Contemplate

The fruit of the Spirit is love, joy, peace, forbearance, kindness, goodness, faithfulness, gentleness, and self-control. (Gal. 5:22–23)

QUESTIONS FOR THE WILDERNESS JOURNAL

1. What kind of fruit is currently growing in your life, and what does that tell you about your spiritual habits?
2. Which of the fruits of the Spirit do you most desire to grow in right now?
3. How much time and discipline have you truly invested in your walk with Jesus?
4. What one small spiritual discipline could you start this week to strengthen your faith? Some of them include daily time in Scripture, solitude, prayer, and fasting.
5. How does your training in other areas of life (e.g., career, hobbies, health) compare to your training in godliness?

PRAYER OF THE DAY

Lord, I want to bear good fruit. I confess that I've expected spiritual growth without investing the time and discipline it takes to know You deeply. Teach me to train with You. Help me pursue You like I pursue other goals—with passion, consistency, and purpose. Shape my character through Your Spirit and grow the fruit in me that honors You. In Jesus's name, amen.

WILDERNESS APPLICATION

- Go for a walk in nature and look specifically for signs of fruit, seeds, or growth. Reflect on what's growing in your own life right now.
- Choose one fruit of the Spirit (love, joy, peace, etc.) and write it down on a slip of paper. Carry it with you all week as a focus for prayer and practice.
- Start a daily discipline log in your journal to track your time spent in prayer, solitude, Scripture, or service.
- Prepare a small patch of soil or plant a seed. As it grows, let it be a reminder that growth takes time, consistency, and care.
- Memorize Galatians 5:22–23 this week, and pray each fruit over yourself every morning.

WILD FOUNDATION

A good shelter can mean the difference between life and death in a wilderness survival situation. It protects from wind, rain, and freezing temperatures. It provides a sense of security and rest when everything else feels uncertain. But no matter how strong or well-built a shelter may be, it's only as reliable as the ground it's built upon.

I'll never forget filming an episode of *Fat Guys in the Woods* for The Weather Channel. We were deep in the Red River Gorge in Kentucky. After hiking for several hours, we stumbled across what seemed to be an ideal location to build our shelter. It was tucked beneath the base of a cliff, protected from the cold March winds, and surrounded by plenty of fir trees, which were perfect for bedding and roofing material.

The four of us invested hours of effort building a lean-to big enough for all of us to fit comfortably. We lined the bed with thick fir boughs and secured the roof tightly. Just as we tied off the final knots, a cold, freezing rain started to fall.

Aside from a few minor leaks, the fir branches kept us dry, and we slept well on our bough beds. But when the sun rose,

I realized we were in trouble, and there was no one to blame but me.

What had looked like a flat, solid area the day before had now become a shallow basin of standing water. The cliffs above us had funneled gallons of rain right down into the very spot we had chosen to set up camp. The ground around our shelter was soaked. A brand-new body of water had formed and was now slowly creeping toward the front of our shelter.

We had unintentionally built on bad ground. We weren't just damp; we were fully camped in a swamp. And the guys were looking at me like *Creek . . . what now?*

Thankfully, the rain stopped, and slowly the water began to soak into the forest floor. Our shelter was still damp and miserable, but at least it wasn't underwater. We recovered from the mistake, and, thankfully, my reputation was spared on national television.

But it left me with a survival lesson I'll never forget: A shelter is only as good as its foundation.

Jesus teaches a parallel truth in Matthew 7:24–27:

> Therefore everyone who hears these words of mine and puts them into practice is like a wise man who built his house on the rock.
>
> The rain came down, the streams rose, and the winds blew and beat against that house; yet it did not fall, because it had its foundation on the rock.
>
> But everyone who hears these words of mine and does not put them into practice is like a foolish man who built his house on sand.
>
> The rain came down, the streams rose, and the winds blew and beat against that house, and it fell with a great crash.

Two builders. Same storm. Different outcomes.

The difference wasn't in the walls, the roofing, or the craftsmanship of the structure.

It was the foundation. Scripture reminds us that Jesus is more than just a firm place to stand, He is the Cornerstone. Ephesians 2:19–20 says this clearly: "Consequently, you are no longer foreigners and strangers, but fellow citizens with God's people and also members of his household, built on the foundation of the apostles and prophets, with Christ Jesus himself as the chief cornerstone."

In ancient times, the cornerstone was the first and most important stone set in place. Every other stone in the structure aligned to it. If it was flawed, the whole building was unstable. But if it was solid and square, the entire structure had integrity.

When everything washes away, Jesus is still there. He is the Rock at the bottom when everything else crumbles.

And unlike that shelter in the wilds of Kentucky, it's never too late to rebuild the shelter of your life on the right foundation. Jesus invites us, no matter how broken or swamped our current structure may be, to tear down what won't last and start again with Him. It's not easy, but it's worth it. When the foundation is right, nothing can knock you out.

Psalm 18:2 puts it like this: "The Lord is my rock, my fortress and my deliverer; my God is my rock, in whom I take refuge."

When Jesus is the Rock beneath you, and the Father is the shelter above you, no storm in this world, physical or spiritual, can take what matters most.

IN THE WILD

Verse to Contemplate

Therefore everyone who hears these words of mine and puts them into practice is like a wise man who built his house on the rock. (Matt. 7:24)

QUESTIONS FOR THE WILDERNESS JOURNAL

1. What parts of your life have you built on sand instead of the Rock?
2. Have you seen any leaks or instability in those areas recently?
3. What would it look like to rebuild that area with Christ as the foundation?
4. Are you willing to tear down something that's not secure in order to build what will last?
5. Where do you need to take refuge in God today?

PRAYER OF THE DAY

Lord Jesus, You are my Rock and my foundation. I confess that I've built parts of my life on other things, such as my plans, my pride, my success, or my own strength. Today I choose to tear those things down and rebuild with You. Be the cornerstone of my heart, my home, my family, and my future. Help me to trust You when the rains come and to know, deep down, that You will never move. In Jesus's name, amen.

WILDERNESS APPLICATION

- Go outside and build a simple survival shelter such as a lean-to, debris hut, or tarp. Before you even begin, look at the ground. Is it flat? Is it in a low spot? Could it collect water? Let that search for solid ground be a spiritual one too. Ask God to show you areas in your life that need a new foundation.
- Find a large rock, sit on it, and read Psalm 18:2 aloud. As you sit, imagine every part of your life—your past, your present, your future—fully resting on Christ.
- Journal a blueprint of your life, including your faith, family, finances, goals, habits, and identity. Circle the areas that are truly built on Jesus. Underline the ones that aren't. Pray over what needs to change.
- Draw or build a cornerstone, label it "Jesus," and place it somewhere you'll see it often, such as your yard, your desk, or your workshop as a reminder of what your life must rest upon.

WILD WATER

There's a saying in the survival world: "You stake your life on your water source." What that means is simple. You'd better be sure your water is safe to drink, because it's a life-and-death decision in the wild.

Water from ponds, creeks, and streams in the wilderness can be contaminated with a variety of microscopic organisms that can make you dangerously sick. These include:

- protozoan cysts like cryptosporidium and giardia
- bacteria such as *E. coli* and *Salmonella*
- viruses like norovirus and hepatitis A

Without access to modern medical care, the vomiting and diarrhea caused by these waterborne illnesses can lead to dehydration, exhaustion, and even death.

There are several ways to make wild water safe to drink. Boiling is 100 percent effective against microbiological organisms. Just bringing water to a rolling boil is sufficient to kill them.

These days, however, small portable water filters are one of the best and easiest ways to make water drinkable in the backcountry. While filters don't *kill* organisms, they're very effective at removing the bad bugs that would otherwise make us sick or worse. I always recommend keeping a portable water filter in your seventy-two-hour bug out bag, your hiking kit, and your camping gear.

Just as filtering wild water is crucial for physical survival, filtering what we allow into our minds and hearts is critical for spiritual survival. Just like dirty water can poison the body, toxic thoughts and influences can poison the soul.

The world, the flesh, and the devil would love to dump spiritual toxins into our thought life. But thankfully, God gives us a filter. Philippians 4:8 is essentially God's checklist for what we should let in, and what we should filter out: "Finally, brothers and sisters, whatever is true, whatever is noble, whatever is right, whatever is pure, whatever is lovely, whatever is admirable—if anything is excellent or praiseworthy—think about such things."

There's a huge misconception in wilderness training: People assume that clear water is clean water, but it's the *invisible stuff* that can hurt you the most. The same is true with thoughts, influences, and behaviors. They might *seem* harmless but can have devastating consequences on your relationship with Jesus.

The patterns of this world are like polluted water. They may be common, but they are not clean. Romans 12:2 tells us to filter the world's messages through God's truth, which is the Word of God: "Do not conform to the pattern of this world, but be transformed by the renewing of your mind. Then you will be able to test and approve what God's will is—his good, pleasing and perfect will."

Your heart is like your body's water source. Whatever enters it affects your entire life. It should be aggressively guarded as Proverbs 4:23 instructs, just like you'd guard your water supply in the wild: "Above all else, guard your heart, for everything you do flows from it."

Living unfiltered, which looks like walking with the wicked, standing with sinners, and sitting with mockers, leads to spiritual dehydration. But filtered living that is rooted in God's Word produces a steady, strong, and fruitful life, like a well-watered tree. Psalm 1:1–3 reminds us of this:

> Blessed is the one
>   who does not walk in step with the wicked
> or stand in the way that sinners take
>   or sit in the company of mockers,
> but whose delight is in the law of the LORD,
>   and who meditates on his law day and night.
> That person is like a tree planted by streams of water,
>   which yields its fruit in season
> and whose leaf does not wither—
>   whatever they do prospers.

The enemy is dumping poisonous toxins into your water source from every angle, including social media, cell phones, television, commercials, entertainment, books, artificial intelligence, and more. If what you're consuming doesn't pass through the filter of "true, noble, right, pure, lovely, admirable, excellent, praiseworthy," then it has no business entering your mind or heart.

Discernment, the ability to recognize what's toxic, is developed through the daily spiritual disciplines of reading Scripture, praying, and spending time alone with God.

Survival in the wilderness may depend on what you filter from your water . . .

But survival in life depends on what you filter from your heart.

IN THE WILD

Verse to Contemplate

> Finally, brothers and sisters, whatever is true, whatever is noble, whatever is right, whatever is pure, whatever is lovely, whatever is admirable—if anything is excellent or praiseworthy—think about such things. (Phil. 4:8)

QUESTIONS FOR THE WILDERNESS JOURNAL

1. What unfiltered influences have I been allowing into my heart and mind lately?
2. Which of the Philippians 4:8 filters do I struggle to apply most?
3. What spiritual disciplines can I practice more consistently to build discernment?

PRAYER OF THE DAY

Lord, I want my mind and heart to be clean. Help me see the invisible toxins that are polluting my thoughts. Teach me to filter everything through Your truth and guard my heart like a wilderness water source. Give me discernment, conviction, and courage to shut out what doesn't belong. In Jesus's name, amen.

WILDERNESS APPLICATION

- Boil or filter water in the wild (or at home), observe what's removed from it, and reflect on the invisible dangers.
- Create your own Philippians 4:8 filter—write down the eight traits (true, noble, right, pure, lovely, admirable, excellent, praiseworthy) and evaluate your inputs for one full day: media, thoughts, conversations, and so on.
- Share one thing with a friend or spiritual mentor that you need to start filtering, and ask for encouragement.

WILD VALLEY

In survival, mountain peaks are the worst places to be. On mountain peaks, resources are scarce. There is typically no food, no water, and no shelter, only snow, rocks, and straggly trees stunted in growth by extreme weather. The best survival strategy is to move down into the valleys as quickly as possible. The valley is where the resources are. Here, you'll find water, vegetation, animals, shelter, and even other people. The valley provides the tools and resources necessary to survive the challenges ahead.

In life, the same truth applies: To survive the peaks, you often need to go into the valleys.

That's where the resources are.

I'll never forget the day we got the call. My wife Sarah and I were in a good place with two young kids, River and Lakelyn. Life was comfortable, until it wasn't. Sarah was fifteen weeks pregnant with our third child, a little girl named Primrose Eve. But the doctors told us she had trisomy 18, a genetic condition labeled "incompatible with life." Our happiness turned to anxiety, our hope to doubt. For seven months, our lives felt like they were on hold.

But we remembered what God had already done for us, as I shared in the devotional about how He restored our marriage. If He could do that, He could do anything. We prayed fervently for a miracle, and dozens of others prayed with us.

The morning Primrose was born, we walked into the hospital believing for a miracle. When she arrived, she was perfect and beautiful. I looked at Sarah and said, "We've got this."

Primrose opened her big brown eyes and stared into mine, as if to tell me everything would be okay.

But it wasn't okay. One moment, we were dreaming of our future with her. The next, we were holding her in our arms, weeping as she took her last breath. She was here, and then she wasn't, and with her went a piece of our hearts. We walked into the hospital with hope and dreams, and we left feeling hopeless. Where was our miracle? Where was God?

We found ourselves in the darkest valley we had ever experienced. But remember what we know about the valleys when it comes to survival? That's where the resources are.

Psalm 34:19 reminds us that God works in all places: "The righteous person may have many troubles, but the Lord delivers him from them all."

I left the hospital a different man. Although we had lost our little girl, I felt the Holy Spirit in that room more than ever before. Amid the heartbreak, there was an overwhelming peace. It sounds strange, but we were both completely empty and completely full at the same time. Our prayer hadn't been answered, but we were not abandoned.

Suddenly, I saw life more clearly. I had surrendered my marriage to Jesus, but I had held tightly to everything else, including my business, my finances, my time, and my influence. But after that day, I didn't want the things of this world anymore. It was as if a light had been turned on, and I saw my life in a new way. Losing our daughter made clear the brevity of life and also made me long for the heaven that God promises.

My wife and I have come to believe that Primrose's death was allowed for a special purpose. Sarah and I had one foot in the world and one foot in the kingdom. We were close to surrendering everything, but I doubt we ever would have without what happened with Primrose. But after Primrose, we no longer had a desire for the things of this world. We craved the eternal in a new and life-changing way. Romans 5:3–5 resonated with us powerfully: "We also glory in our sufferings, because we know that suffering produces perseverance; perseverance, character; and character, hope. And hope does not put us to shame, because God's love has been poured out into our hearts through the Holy Spirit, who has been given to us."

Primrose lived for four hours, never speaking a word, but her life changed the course of mine. Her brief time with us became the catalyst for a complete shift in focus from the fleeting things of this world to the unseen treasures of eternity. Just like people in survival stories, I found the resources I needed in the valley. That valley is much of the reason why you're reading this devotional today.

God uses the valleys to forge character, faith, and resilience. The hard times help us focus on what really matters, and they strip away the distractions that keep us from real sustenance. The valleys are where the survival resources in life are found.

These are faith, perseverance, and resilience. And those resources can change eternity.

We don't usually go looking for valleys. They often find us. And when they do, it's easy to feel like we've been abandoned or forgotten. But what if the valley isn't a punishment but rather a preparation? What if it's not the end but the beginning of a deeper faith? God doesn't waste pain. He meets us in the lowest places with the deepest truths. If you're in a valley right now, don't run from it. Instead, lean into what God might be doing in you. The resources are there, waiting.

IN THE WILD

Verses to Contemplate

> We also glory in our sufferings, because we know that suffering produces perseverance; perseverance, character; and character, hope. And hope does not put us to shame, because God's love has been poured out into our hearts through the Holy Spirit, who has been given to us. (Rom. 5:3–5)

QUESTIONS FOR THE WILDERNESS JOURNAL

1. What valley are you walking through right now or have you walked through recently?
2. In what ways has God met you in that valley, even if your prayers weren't answered how you hoped?

3. What resources (e.g., faith, clarity, humility, hope) has the valley given you?
4. Are there areas of your life you're still holding on to instead of surrendering to God?
5. How can you honor someone's life, or a painful experience, by the way you live?

PRAYER OF THE DAY

Father, the valley is painful, but I know You are here. Even when my prayers go unanswered, help me trust that You are working for my good and Your glory. I give You the pieces of my pain and ask You to shape them into something eternal. Teach me to see with eyes of faith and help me honor You with my story. Thank You for meeting me in the valley. I'm listening. In Jesus's name, amen.

WILDERNESS APPLICATION

- Go on a slow, quiet walk in a low place, such as along a creek bed, a wooded trail, or a quiet valley, and reflect on the idea that valleys are places of growth and provision.
- Sit outside at dusk or dawn, times that reflect transition, and journal about what God is refining in you right now.
- Choose a stone and carry it with you throughout the day. Let it represent both the weight of grief and the strength of what God is building in you.

WILD FORGE

There's something beautiful, and brutal, about forging a knife.

I remember the first time I used a cheaply made knife on a wilderness survival course early in my career. It looked great on the outside, but the first time I batoned it through a thick log, the blade snapped clean in half in front of over thirty students. That knife hadn't been forged. It had been shaped but never tested. And when it mattered, it failed. I learned the hard way the difference between a knife that has been through the forge and one that hasn't.

To forge a knife, the metal must endure intense heat. It must be pounded, shaped, and hammered again and again. It starts as a raw, unremarkable piece of steel. On its own, it's useless in battle and unfit for true purpose. But in the hands of a skilled blacksmith, that steel becomes something entirely different. It is transformed into something strong, sharp, and able to stand up to serious testing. Not in spite of the fire but because of it.

Then the knife is quenched—plunged into oil or water. This quenching process hardens the steel but makes it brittle. After the initial forging and hardening, the blade still isn't ready. It needs to be tempered. This involves reheating the blade at a lower temperature to reduce brittleness. Without tempering, a blade is prone to breaking. Without fire, it's weak. It's a relentless process of controlled pressure and purpose.

Which knife would you rather have in a wilderness survival scenario—one that looks good on the outside or one that's been through the fire and is ready for battle?

What kind of knife are you?

If you haven't figured it out yet, you're just like that piece of steel, and God is the blacksmith. God doesn't want to see your life snap under pressure. He wants you to endure, and that means you have to go through the fire first. Isaiah 48:10 says it this way: "See, I have refined you, though not as silver; I have tested you in the furnace of affliction."

We often think that pain is punishment, but in God's hands, pain has purpose. We are refined, not rejected, in the heat of life's hardest seasons. James 1:2–4 urges us to "consider it pure joy, my brothers and sisters, whenever you face trials of many kinds, because you know that the testing of your faith produces perseverance. Let perseverance finish its work so that you may be mature and complete, not lacking anything."

Testing produces strength. And God doesn't allow the hammer to fall without shaping something in us. But God doesn't just throw us into trials and leave us there. He walks with us through seasons of fire, then gently brings us into seasons of healing and recalibration, a spiritual tempering. The goal isn't to break us, it's to build something balanced, strong, and useful.

First Peter 1:6–7 outlines this principle clearly: "In all this you greatly rejoice, though now for a little while you may have had to suffer grief in all kinds of trials. These have come so that the proven genuineness of your faith—of greater worth than gold, which perishes even though refined by fire—may result in praise, glory and honor when Jesus Christ is revealed." God doesn't waste pain. He uses the fire to shape us, the pounding to strengthen us, and the testing to reveal what we're made of.

The trials in your life aren't signs that God has abandoned you, they're signs that He's forming you for a greater purpose. Your valley, your loss, your unanswered prayer, your disappointment—they're all part of the forge.

The truth is a blade can't be trusted unless it's been tested. Neither can our faith. Sometimes, we're going to fail. I've failed. Some of my biggest regrets are from moments when I've failed a test of my faith, done something out of character, compromised my integrity, or fallen short of God's expectations for me. But those are also the moments that God has used to shape me the most. Failure does not equal brokenness, and it does not mean the tool cannot still be used.

Scripture is full of people forged by fire. Hagar was cast out into the wilderness with her son, but it was there that she encountered God and was promised her child would become a great nation. Mary bore shame and heartbreak, but through her trust in the midst of theoretical flames, God brought the Savior of the world into being. Even Jesus didn't begin His ministry until He had walked through the wilderness where He was tempted by Satan. God always prepares His vessels through hardship. The forging precedes the calling. Sometimes the hardship is a direct consequence of our actions, and sometimes it just happens.

So if you feel like the heat is on and the blows just keep coming, take heart. You're not being destroyed. You're being shaped. God is forming something in you that will help you stand through storms, resist temptation, and be ready for battle. He's not after your comfort, He's after your strength. And He's after your heart.

Maybe you're in the fire right now. Maybe life has felt like one hard blow after another, with loss, disappointment, anxiety, burnout, and unanswered prayers. It's easy to believe God is distant in those seasons. But what if He's right there at the anvil, lovingly forming you for a purpose you can't yet see? What if what feels like a breakdown is actually a buildup?

Second Corinthians 4:17–18 helps put our troubles into perspective: "For our light and momentary troubles are achieving for us an eternal glory that far outweighs them all. So we fix our eyes not on what is seen, but on what is unseen, since what is seen is temporary, but what is unseen is eternal."

A forged blade isn't made to stay on display. It's made for the field. For the mission. For the fight. That's what God is shaping in you. A life that doesn't break under pressure. A faith that cuts through lies. A spirit ready to stand strong for the kingdom of God.

When Jesus returns, the testing of your faith won't be wasted. It will shine. It will bring glory to God. And that's a promise!

The fire is real. But so is your purpose.

You may not be able to control the fire, but you can choose how you respond to it. If you're feeling the heat right now, don't rush out of the forge. Instead, lean into what God is doing in you.

IN THE WILD

Verse to Contemplate

See, I have refined you, though not as silver; I have tested you in the furnace of affliction. (Isa. 48:10)

QUESTIONS FOR THE WILDERNESS JOURNAL

1. What current or past trial in your life feels like a forge?
2. Have you ever mistaken God's refining process for punishment? What shifted your perspective?
3. In what ways has your faith been tested? How did you respond?
4. What part of your life still needs to be surrendered to the forge—tempered, shaped, and made strong?
5. What strength, character, or insight has come from a season of fire in your life?

PRAYER OF THE DAY

Father, I don't always understand the fire, but I trust You as the blacksmith. Shape me, strengthen me, and don't stop until I become who You created me to be. Help me endure the blows, embrace the heat, and hold tightly to the truth that You are with me through every trial. I give You full permission to forge me for Your purpose. In Jesus's name, amen.

WILDERNESS APPLICATION

- Spend time outdoors by a campfire or in front of a fireplace. Reflect on how fire transforms what it touches. Ask God what He wants to refine in you.
- Go on a hike with a trusted forged tool, like a knife, and think about its journey to usefulness. What parallels do you see in your own spiritual walk?
- Sketch or journal a picture of your forge season. What has God hammered away? What is He shaping?
- Write a note to your future self while in wilderness solitude. Having been through the forge, what do you want your future self to remember about God's faithfulness in the fire?

WILD EMBER

Fire is the king of all survival tools. With it, you can regulate your core body temperature, boil water, cook food, stave off predators, make tools, and signal for rescue. And if you're lost and alone in the wilderness, fire can be your best friend.

I can start a fire over one hundred different ways, but one of my favorites to teach students in my WILD GOD survival courses is the bow drill. Like I mentioned before, the bow drill method involves spinning a spindle into a hearth board to generate a small, fragile ember of smoldering wood dust. It's a combination of pressure and speed and requires a great deal of patience and technique to master. I've taught thousands of students all over the world how to make fire with the bow drill.

But the goal isn't just to generate a smoldering ember. The ember is just the beginning. The ultimate goal is to place that ember into a prepared tinder bundle and blow it into a flame.

The ember is created with one plan and purpose in mind—fire.

Alone, the ember represents only potential. It has the possibility for greatness, but when exposed to the elements, it can quickly die out and become a cold pile of ash. Alone, it cannot boil water, provide warmth, or signal for rescue. It has no lasting impact and can disappear as quickly as it arrives with the slightest gust of cold wind or a single drop of water.

Unless the creator of that ember gently places it into a tinder bundle and skillfully coaxes it to flame, it has no hope of realizing the purpose it was designed for.

In and of themselves, embers are weak. But in the hands of a knowledgeable creator, they have the potential to save lives, transform landscapes, provide light, and warm a frigid soul.

An ember must be surrendered to step into its true purpose. There is no other way.

Depending on the circumstances, some embers take more time than others. The conditions have a lot to do with it. Is the tinder dry? Is it raining? Is there wind? Is it cold? Is the environment difficult?

But I've learned that in the hands of a skilled fire starter, *all* embers can be transformed into fire, regardless of the situation.

I want you to contemplate for a couple of minutes what Colossians 3:9–10 says: "Do not lie to each other, since you have taken off your old self with its practices and have put on the new self, which is being renewed in knowledge in the image of its Creator."

Embers can't burst into flame on their own. They can only do so in the skilled hands of the Creator. The Lord who has ignited the ember within you has the desire, plan, and ability to finish what He has started, just as Psalm 139:13–16 reminds us:

> For you created my inmost being;
> you knit me together in my mother's womb.

> I praise you because I am fearfully and wonderfully made;
>   your works are wonderful,
>   I know that full well.
> My frame was not hidden from you
>   when I was made in the secret place,
>   when I was woven together in the depths of the earth.
> Your eyes saw my unformed body;
>   all the days ordained for me were
> written in your book
>   before one of them came to be.

When an ember is taken to flame, it is under complete surrender to the Creator. The Lord owns the fire and works in and through us to achieve His perfect will. When we surrender the ember of our soul to the One who made it, we make the decision to be engulfed by and used by Him entirely.

We become a part of the fire, but it is His fire to use for His purpose.

His will becomes our will. Everything we are becomes God's flame: our gifts, talents, relationships, careers, time, land, finances, experiences, failures, and successes. God doesn't want 10 percent of our ember, He wants it all. That is what full flame requires.

John 15:5 explains it like this: "I am the vine; you are the branches. If you remain in me and I in you, you will bear much fruit; apart from me you can do nothing." With this perspective, we must be *all in*. We are no longer slaves to the things of this world, such as careers, money, and even our own dreams. These things make terrible masters and will never satisfy. But when we place them all in the tinder bundle, all of them serve a greater purpose: to glorify God.

I spent forty years of my life not understanding this concept, only surrendering parts of my ember. I lived enslaved to my own ideas and the world's definitions of success. As a survival instructor, I should have realized earlier that surrendering the full ember is necessary. There is overwhelming peace when you hand over everything to Someone more skilled, more loving, and far more capable than you. Someone who knows the purpose, even when you may not. The writer of Psalm 24:1 knew this: "The earth is the LORD's, and everything in it, the world, and all who live in it."

The ember, in its entirety, is now a part of something bigger, more powerful, more meaningful, and more impactful than it could ever be alone. God can and will use the fire ignited from your ember to shape eternity, just as a survivor uses fire in the wilderness for shelter, warmth, and rescue. The irony is that we must choose to relinquish that ember back to Him. Matthew 5:14–16 challenges us to do just that: "You are the light of the world. A town built on a hill cannot be hidden. Neither do people light a lamp and put it under a bowl. Instead they put it on its stand, and it gives light to everyone in the house. In the same way, let your light shine before others, that they may see your good deeds and glorify your Father in heaven."

The question we must all ask ourselves is this:

What will we do with our ember?

Will we let it die, exposed to the elements of the world, never becoming what it was meant to be?

Will we fan it just enough to keep it alive, but never surrender it fully, never stepping into the flame of our true purpose?

Or will we place it completely into the hands of the One who created it, trusting Him to breathe life into it and ignite a fire that burns for His glory?

Your ember was created with intention. But flame only comes through surrender.

IN THE WILD

Verse to Contemplate

I have been crucified with Christ and I no longer live, but Christ lives in me. The life I now live in the body, I live by faith in the Son of God, who loved me and gave himself for me. (Gal. 2:20)

QUESTIONS FOR THE WILDERNESS JOURNAL

1. Does your life feel like a smoldering ember right now? Are you full of potential, but at risk of burning out?
2. In what ways have you tried to ignite your own fire apart from God? What were the results?
3. What would it look like to fully surrender your ember to the hands of your Creator today?
4. Are you holding back part of your life from God's flame? Why?
5. What has God already ignited in you that could be used to bring warmth, light, and hope to others?

PRAYER OF THE DAY

Lord Jesus, I surrender the ember of my soul into Your hands. I know You created me with purpose, and I want to burn for You. I no longer want to hold back or smolder in fear. Blow Your breath over the ember within me and ignite it into a flame for Your glory. Use every part of me. I surrender my past, my present, and my future for Your will and not my own. I trust You as the One who formed me, saved me, and now calls me to burn brightly in a dark world. In Jesus's name, amen.

WILDERNESS APPLICATION

- Go outside and practice building a small fire from scratch. Use flint, a ferro rod, or even a bow drill, if you're able. As you work, reflect on the patience and care required to grow an ember into flame. Ask God to do the same with your heart.
- Find a quiet natural spot, close your eyes, and imagine God breathing gently on the ember of your soul. What is He inviting you to ignite?
- Sketch the process of fire starting in your journal, including the hearth board, ember, tinder bundle, and flame. Label the parts with areas of your life (e.g., calling, giftedness, fear, surrender).
- Take a photo of a flame or candle and save it as your lock screen to remind you daily: Your life was created to burn for something bigger.

- While taking solitude in the wild, write a letter to God titled "My Ember." Tell Him what you're surrendering and what you hope He sets ablaze.

CONCLUSION

Creation is an extension of how we can experience, learn from, and engage with our Creator through His Word and His world. As Romans 1:20 reminds us, "For since the creation of the world God's invisible qualities—his eternal power and divine nature—have been clearly seen, being understood from what has been made, so that people are without excuse." Creation speaks loudly of God's order, control, majesty, and provision. It is both a testimony of His glory and a living sermon that leaves us without excuse.

As the first venue God chose to dwell in with humanity, the wilderness is full of infinite provision lessons and spiritual parallels that strengthen our faith and deepen our relationship with the Creator. God hardwired truth into every leaf, every rock, every tree, and every creature. It's all for His glory and for our provision, reflection, and joy.

The relationship between God and humanity began in the wild. And no number of buildings, temples, stained-glass windows, or fancy churches will ever replace the unique and sacred connection that exists when we spend time with God in the wilderness.

God's wildness is not only evident in the unfiltered dynamics of creation, but also in the untamed and unpredictable ways He moves in our lives. Just as we can't comprehend the size of a galaxy, we also cannot fully understand the scale of His plan as it unfolds through our individual stories. But oh, what an honor it is to be part of it.

One thing is for certain: When we deny ourselves the connection to God in the wild that our soul craves, the fire within us slowly begins to burn to ash. Our faith becomes cold, distant, and fragile.

But take heart: He's still there.

Just like He did with Adam and Eve, He still walks in the garden in the cool of the day, and He will walk with you too. But you must go meet Him there.

And who knows? He might just reveal a survival skill or two along the way.

I hope to see you at a WILD GOD event soon.

God is wild!

CREEK STEWART is a world-renowned wilderness survival instructor, author, keynote speaker, and television host who has spent his career teaching others how to thrive in the wild. He is the author of more than forty books, including *Disaster Survival 101* and *Build the Perfect Bug Out Bag*. He's the in-house survival expert for The Weather Channel, as well as the host of several internationally syndicated survival shows, including his newest television show, *GOD IN THE WILD*. Now, through his WILD GOD ministry, Creek helps people encounter Jesus and grow deeper in relationship with Him through time in God's creation.

CONNECT WITH CREEK

WildGod.org and CreekStewart.com

@CreekStewart

@CreekStewart